50 Great Dis

By Human Folly

Jeffrey L. King

PUBLISHING

CSJ King Publishing, LLC

Oregon, Wisconsin

Copyright © 2016 CSJ King Publishing, LLC

ISBN: 0985622040

ISBN-13: 978-0-9856220-4-6

Dedication

This work is dedicated to all those souls, through the millennia, who have lost their lives needlessly due to human folly. Your sacrifice is acknowledged; your death is mourned. The human condition improves because of you.

Acknowledgments

First, I have to thank my coworkers, Mike and Mike and Beth, for being there and planting the seed which became this book. Thanks to my wife, Didi; when I came to her with this idea, she encouraged me and thought it was a good project to embark upon. My proofreaders, Mike Woodard and Didi King, get credit for ensuring this book meets their standards of perfection. Thank you to my daughter Cassie, a published author, for inspiration and showing me that this project was doable. And thanks to my other children, Sydney and Jackson, for listening to my tales with interest, and for tolerating my long hours researching and writing.

Table of Contents

Foreword

human folly [fol-ee]

noun

definition:

1. Lack of good sense, understanding, or foresight.

2. An act or instance of foolishness.

3. A costly undertaking having an absurd or ruinous outcome.

In the grand scheme of the history of the universe, humans have existed for only the briefest of recent moments. In that short time, we have evolved from hunters and gatherers to farmers to mass food producers; from simple tool makers to industrial workers; from believers of sorcery and superstition to scientists. Humans have traded hand carving tools and subsistence labor for communication and technology on a grand scale. In this short time, we've gone from making crude shelters out of what we could scavenge from nature, to technology that allows us to communicate instantly with anyone, anywhere, and to even leave our home planet.

But, for all the advancements we have made, one thing has never changed: our propensity to engage in acts of folly. We act out of emotion, or greed, or ignorance, and someone pays the price. We make poor decisions that lack insight, and someone pays the price. We regularly fail to learn from our previous mistakes, and someone pays the price. We react to events without everyone's best interest in mind, and someone pays the price. We think of other humans as unworthy, or dispensable, or as the means to an end, and they often pay the price.

This collection of historical tales has its genesis in conversations at work over lunch. Conversations often turned to stupid things humans do, whether it's on the freeway during the morning commute, or in the realm of politics. In time, instances of foolish things humans have done to create a large-scale disaster, or to make a natural disaster even worse, entered the conversation, and the idea for this book was born.

I've always had a fascination with disasters, and remember as a child checking out every book from the local library on the subject. Now, with the prevalence of the Internet and personal devices with cameras carried by nearly everyone, there are plenty of disasters or near-disasters caught on film. Nearly every day, these videos make their way into television newscasts. And there is a demand for it, obviously, or we wouldn't see it on our screens every day. Who doesn't stop what they are doing to watch the latest disaster footage? Isn't everyone glad it's someone else? Maybe it's just me, but I don't think so.

I've chosen fifty disasters, some well-known, others you probably haven't ever heard of, and laid out a narrative of the event. They span the last two centuries or so in time. In some, only a handful of people died (and in a couple, there were no fatalities), but the death toll in others reached staggering proportions, some with hundreds of thousands of deaths. With many volumes already written about history's great disasters, I attempted to focus on those events that were created or exacerbated by human folly. There were plenty to choose from.

One thing that I chose not to do in this book was to focus on the human drama in depth. While any disaster that takes a human toll is unfortunate, it is important to understand the experiences and emotions of those directly involved. Most of the disasters presented here have had numerous entire volumes written about the event, often containing interviews with survivors regarding the reality of the situation. For space purposes, I have not included very many witness statements; if I had, this volume could have easily been 1,000 pages long. Instead, I will leave it to the reader, if interested, to further investigate each disaster in greater detail. My goal here is to provide an overview of each disaster and explain how human folly made the event worse.

The absurdity of some of these disasters may make you snicker. Nearly all of these disasters are forehead slappers. What were they thinking? How could they think that decision would turn out well? Couldn't they see what the consequences of their actions might be? But humans do not learn to protect ourselves, and especially others, quickly. Mass deaths by fire or ferry sinkings continue to be headlines around the world today, although we already have the knowledge and means to prevent these from occurring on the scale and frequency they still do.

I discuss some well-known events, such as the Chernobyl nuclear disaster, of which you undoubtedly are at least somewhat familiar. You will also read about some rather obscure disasters you have probably never heard of, because they have been nearly lost to history, or they occurred in part of the world where information dissemination is not a priority. I saved the "best" for last; a disaster of biblical proportions that involves earthquake, fire, tsunami, typhoon, landslides, a fire tornado, and—of course—genocide.

This is the part of the foreword where I would normally invite you to enjoy your reading experience, but if you are like me, you'll cringe more than you will enjoy this collection of stories. So be it. If we fail to learn from our previous mistakes, we will continue to have fires, structural collapses, explosions, crashes, industrial accidents, or maritime disasters that result in a great loss of human life.

"If each man *or woman could understand that every other human life is as full of sorrows, or joys, or base temptations, of heartaches and of remorse as his own . . . how much kinder, how much gentler he would be."* — William Allen White, American journalist (1868-1944)

1

Great Molasses Flood

1919

Massachusetts, USA

> *"Here and there struggled a form—whether it was animal or human being was impossible to tell. Only an upheaval, a thrashing about in the sticky mass, showed where any life was ... Horses died like so many flies on sticky fly-paper. The more they struggled, the deeper in the mess they were ensnared. Human beings—men and women—suffered likewise."* —Boston Post report

Some disasters are so bizarre that mentioning them in a conversation evokes giggles and questions about whether or not it ever actually happened. The Great Molasses Flood in Boston, Massachusetts, is one of these unbelievable disasters.

On January 15, 1919, a huge molasses tank split open and spilled its contents, creating a 25-foot (7.6-meter) wave of sticky goo, moving through the streets at as much as 35 miles per hour (56 kilometers per hour). Twenty-one people were overtaken by the wave and died; 150 others were injured.

Molasses is a by-product of refining sugarcane or sugar beets into sugar. The viscous substance can be fermented to make rum, ethanol, and in World War I, it was used in munitions.

The Purity Distilling Company tank and offices were located in Boston's North End neighborhood, near the intersection of Commercial and Charter streets; a baseball diamond and Longone Park now occupy the spot. The enormous molasses tank measured 50 feet (15 m) tall and 90 feet (27 m) in diameter; it could hold 2.3 million gallons (8.7 million liters). Later inquiries revealed that basic safety tests, such as filling the tank with water to test for leaks, were never done. In fact, the tank leaked so much molasses from the very beginning that local residents collected it for personal use, and the owners painted it brown in an attempt to hide the leaks. Local authorities never issued permits or conducted inspections of the enormous tank. Modern engineering studies indicate that the steel used in the tank was only half as thick as it should have been for a tank of that size. In 2015, another study showed that the tank was manufactured from a type of steel susceptible to fracturing; the same type of steel was used in the *Titanic*'s construction.

Other factors played into the disaster. The tank was filled to capacity with a shipment from Puerto Rico as a last-minute effort to make and sell as much rum as possible before Prohibition kicked in (the 18th Amendment was ratified the day after the disaster). The pressure inside the tank had built up that day due to fermentation, which produced carbon dioxide, combined with a quick rise in outside air temperatures (2 to 41°F/-17 to 5°C). The tank had also only been filled to capacity eight times since it had been built in 1916, putting intermittent stress on the structure. A manhole near the tank's base, where pressure is greatest, failed; a fracture appeared, causing the tank to burst.

Witnesses reported the collapse was accompanied by a loud rumbling sound that shook the ground, as well as machine gun-like popping as the rivets that held the tank together shot out. Two 10-year-old children, collecting leaking molasses at the base of the tank, were killed. The ensuing wave destroyed girders of an adjacent elevated

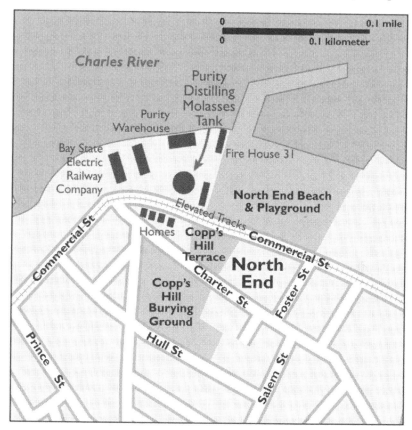

railway, seconds after a train had passed by. Nearby buildings were knocked off their foundations or crushed altogether. The rush of air blew people off their feet. A truck was hurled into Boston Harbor. A neighboring fire house was crushed, killing one fireman.

As the wave subsided, several blocks were flooded two to three feet (60 to 90 cm) deep. People, dogs, and horses alike struggled to escape the sticky mass, which was likened to being stuck to flypaper. One house on Copps Hill was sucked back down into the street by the receding tide of syrup.

9

The USS *Nantucket*, a Massachusetts Nautical School training ship, was docked a couple of blocks away. Lieutenant Commander H. J. Copeland and 116 cadets were the first responders to arrive at the scene. They worked crowd control, to keep the curious from entering the goo and getting stuck too; they also helped pull survivors to safety. More rescuers arrived: the Boston Police, the Red Cross, as well as other military units stationed nearby. It took four days to wade through the molasses and remove the victim's bodies; they were so covered in thick goo it was hard to recognize the bodies.

Cleanup of the area took weeks. Salt water was sprayed from fire boats to wash the molasses into the bay. Rescue workers and the curious had also tracked molasses all over the city, leaving the sticky mess everywhere they went. Central Boston smelled like molasses for decades.

United States Industrial Alcohol Company (USIA) had purchased Purity Distilling in 1917, and they were the target of one of Massachusetts' first class-action lawsuits. After three years of hearings, USIA was found responsible despite their claims that anarchists had blown up the tank. USIA paid out $600,000 in out-of-court settlements.

Locals commemorate the disaster with a historical marker. Boston Duck Tours has also named one of their World War II amphibious tour craft *Molly Molasses* and painted her dark brown.

Although the Great Molasses Flood disaster is certainly an oddity, there have been similar events. A faulty pipeline spilled 1,400 tons of molasses into Honolulu Harbor in Hawaii in 2013, causing widespread environmental damage and killing all sea life in the harbor. In 1814, a large vat of beer in London ruptured; the beer wave destroyed several homes and killed eight.

2

Lac-Mégantic Rail Disaster

2013

Québec, Canada

> *"It was moving at a hellish speed ... no lights, no signals, nothing at all. There was no warning. It was a black blob that came out of nowhere. I realized they were oil tankers and they were going to blow up, so I yelled that to my friends and I got out of there. If we had stayed where we were, we would have been roasted."* —Gilles Fluet, Musi-Café patron

Lac-Mégantic, Québec, with a population of about 6,000, lies about 10 miles inside Canada, across the border from Maine. On July 6, 2013, a runaway freight train derailed and laid waste to the town's central business district, in a classic case of human folly leading to mass death and destruction.

The rail line through Lac-Mégantic was built in the late 1880s to finish the Canadian Pacific Railway's (CPR) transcontinental network, by connecting Montréal, Québec, and Saint John, New Brunswick, through Maine. The line was purchased and has been operated by the United States-based Montreal, Maine and Atlantic Railway (MMA) since 2003. The rail line passes through central Lac-Mégantic; a proposal in the 1970s to bypass the central business district was never implemented because of the costs involved.

When MMA took over the line in January 2003, they implemented a significant cost-cutting strategy which changed train operations and deferred maintenance on existing tracks. Many of the rail lines were in such poor condition by 2013 that speed limits on some segments had been reduced to 10 mph (16 kph). In the yards at nearby Sherbrooke, trains were not allowed to travel more than 5 mph (8 kph). MMA chose not to take advantage of matching funds for infrastructure improvement offered by the provincial and federal governments. This decision would prove to be a fatal mistake.

On the night of July 5–6, 2013, a freight train heading east along the line stopped in Nantes, about seven miles (11 km) west of Lac-Mégantic. The train was 4,701 feet (1,433 m) long and consisted of five locomotives, one control car for the engineer, one loaded box car, and 72 tank cars, each filled with 30,000 gallons (113,000 liters) of crude oil. The oil originated in the Bakken oil field of North Dakota and was destined for an oil refinery in Saint John, New Brunswick.

The tank cars were DOT-111 cars, which according to the National Transportation Safety Board, "have a high incidence of tank failures during accidents." The board in 2009 had cited the model as a factor in a rail accident near Rockford, Illinois, and called their design inadequate. Starting in 2011, Canadian regulations required new tank cars to be built better, although older models were still allowed to be used. Attempts in the U.S. to require replacement of the model were delayed due to lobbying from the transportation and petroleum industries, citing cost.

By July 2012, Canadian regulations allowed MMA to operate Single Person Train Operations (SPTO) in another cost-cutting move by the company. This meant that the trains passing through Lac-Mégantic, with an average of 80 tank cars, carried only one person to oversee operations. In the nine months before the Lac-Mégantic rail disaster, 67 trains containing 3,830 tank cars of Bakken crude passed through the town, with only one person on each train.

All rail cars have two types of brake systems. Air brakes are supplied with air from a compressor in the locomotive. Each car and locomotive on a train are linked with an air brake pipe. When a locomotive is shut off, the compressor no longer supplies air to the system. Also, if there is a leak, air pressure drops and eventually the air brakes fail to work. Each rail car also has at least one hand brake; these mechanical brakes apply brake shoes to the wheels to prevent them from moving. The TSB later determined that between 17 and 26 cars on this particular train would have needed the hand brakes applied in order to keep the train from moving, depending on the amount of force manually applied.

Eight months earlier, the lead locomotive on the train that night was repaired following an engine failure. There was pressure to return the locomotive to service quickly and avoid the cost and time needed for repairs, so the engine was inadequately repaired. The material used to repair it failed, leading to engine surges which created black and white smoke, which on occasion would pour from the locomotive.

The train stopped in Nantes for a scheduled shift change and crew rotation at about 11:00 p.m. At Nantes ,there was a railroad siding (a short stretch of railroad track off the main line used to store railroad cars when not in use). Because the siding contained empty boxcars used by a particleboard manufacturer in Lac-Mégantic, the train was parked on the main line, which was unusual but did not break any regulations. That particular siding is outfitted with a device to prevent trains from rolling onto the main line.

The engineer, Thomas Harding, followed standard procedures and shut down four of the five locomotives. He left the main locomotive running to supply air pressure to the train's air brakes. The TSB later determined that manual hand brakes were applied to the five locomotives, the control car, and the buffer car, but none of the tank cars. When the engineer did the brake test, he incorrectly left the air brakes engaged, leading to the incorrect conclusion that the hand brakes alone would prevent the train from rolling away. Incidentally, Transport Canada had repeatedly reprimanded MMA between 2004 and 2012 for violating handbrake requirements in Nantes, but no fines were ever levied for the infractions.

The engineer contacted the rail traffic controller in Farnham, Québec, and reported the train was secured. He also contacted the rail traffic controller in Bangor, Maine, who was in control of train movements east of Lac-Mégantic, and reported that the main locomotive was having mechanical problems and had been unable to maintain speed, and smoke was emanating from it. The controller and engineer agreed that the problem would be addressed in the morning, when a new engineer was scheduled to continue east with the train.

The engineer followed MMA's plan to leave the train parked on the main line, unattended, with the locomotive cab unlocked and accessible to the general public alongside a highway. Unfortunately, there were no rules prohibiting any of this, even if the train contained hazardous cargo or was parked on a hill.

Despite the fact that the locomotive was left running and was belching oil and thick smoke, the engineer summoned a taxi. The driver later testified that the locomotive was spewing enough oil from its engines that droplets of oil covered the engineer and the taxi's windshield. They departed to a hotel in downtown Lac-Mégantic.

[For an interesting take on the disaster in real time, listen to the actual recordings of phone conversations between the engineer and controllers, both before and after the disaster, at http://www.theglobeandmail.com/news/national/dispatches-from-a-disaster/article20148699/#dashboard/follows/]

At around 10:45, local townspeople noticed the train was in distress but unattended. Thick diesel smoke was reducing visibility on the nearby highway, and a broken piston in the engine was causing sparks to be emitted from the exhaust system.

The locomotive spewed enough oil that it started accumulating under the engine, where it overheated and caught fire. A 911 call was placed at 11:50 for a fire in the main locomotive. A police officer from Lac-Mégantic and the Nantes Fire Department responded. Following protocol, they shut down the diesel engine in the burning locomotive to stop the circulation of fuel feeding the fire. They then extinguished the blaze and notified the rail traffic controller.

Instead of sending the engineer back to the train, MMA sent two track maintenance employees from Lac-Mégantic, who arrived by 12:13 a.m. The foreman was unfamiliar with the air brake system, and when the fire department left, notified the controller that the train was safe.

Because the locomotive had been shut down, air was no longer supplied to the air brake system. By 12:56, enough air had leaked out of the brakes to allow the train to start rolling downhill toward Lac-Mégantic, which lies about 360 feet (110 m) lower than Nantes. Witnesses later reported seeing the train rolling downhill without lights. The track was not equipped to alert the rail traffic controller of a runaway train.

By 1:14 a.m., the train reached downtown Lac-Mégantic, traveling at 65 mph (105 kph). The speed limit there was 10 mph (16 kph). When it reached the at-grade crossing at Frontenac Street, Lac-Mégantic's main street, 63 tank cars and the buffer car derailed. Many of the derailed tank cars split open; about 1.5 million gallons (6 million liters) of crude oil was spilled, and fire broke out.

The locomotives and control car stopped about half a mile (800 m) east of the derailment, where the line started up an incline; the last nine tank cars remained on the track. Over the next hour-and-a-half, while evacuation efforts were underway, the first few locomotives, which had separated from the others and travelled 475 feet (145 m) further, rolled backwards and re-coupled with the trailing section. The locomotives then rolled back toward the disaster site another 106 feet (32 m) before they were secured by re-tightening the hand brakes at about 3:30 a.m.

Derailed and burning tank cars.

Witnesses in downtown Lac-Mégantic reported the train moving at excessive speed, emitting sparks from the wheels, and making a terrible noise. Patrons on the terrace of a bar, Musi-Café, located next to the derailment, watched the tank cars derail, and a wave of spilled oil created a fireball three times as tall as the downtown buildings. Four to six huge explosions shook the town; heat from the flames could be felt more than a mile (1.6 km) away. People in the central business district jumped from second- and third-story windows to escape the inferno. As the burning oil entered the downtown and moved toward the lake, it flowed into the storm sewers, which caused towering flames to emanate from storm sewer drains and manholes.

Firefighters, numbering about 150, were called in from as far away as Sherbrooke, Québec, and Franklin County, Maine. The Lac-Mégantic fire department and other first responders used a rail car mover to pull the nine cars that remained on the tracks away from the inferno. By early afternoon, the fire was contained and stopped spreading. One thousand residents were evacuated initially, and another 1,000 were evacuated later in the day due to toxic fumes. The blast radius was approximately 0.6 miles (1 km) across.

Twenty hours after the initial explosions, the central core of the fire was still inaccessible to firefighters. The fire was finally extinguished after burning for nearly two days.

The Lac-Mégantic derailment site following the accident.

Forty-two bodies were recovered; five more were never found and may have been vaporized in the initial blast.

More than 30 buildings (nearly half the central business district) were destroyed. All but three of the remaining 39 buildings have been demolished because of oil contamination. Fifty-three vehicles were destroyed in the inferno. The town suffered further because of lost businesses, a shut-down of the water supply, and the severed rail line, which was not reopened until December.

The safety record of MMA's parent company, Rail World Inc., was immediately scrutinized. Over the previous decade, the railroad had recorded 36.1 accidents per million miles travelled, compared to a national average of 14.6. One of the company's rail accidents had caused a derailment and fire involving hazardous materials which had burned for more than two weeks in Weyauwega, Wisconsin, in 1996. In August 2013, shortly after the disaster, MMA filed for bankruptcy protection. On December 18, 2013, MMA was allowed to once again operate trains on the line through Lac-Mégantic, although with numerous restrictions, including a prohibition of transporting hazardous materials, no more single-person crews, and an observance of the speed limit of 10 mph (16 kph).

The rail industry has made a number of regulation and policy changes since the Lac-Mégantic disaster. Because of public outcry, Canadian Pacific Railway and Canadian National Railway have announced that they will no longer leave trains unattended or unlocked outside a rail yard, and tank cars containing hazardous materials will no longer be parked on main lines. Single-person crews are now prohibited in Canada, although they are still allowed in the U.S.

The Transportation Safety Board of Canada released its report on the disaster in August 2014, and listed 18 specific causes and contributing factors:

- mechanical troubles with the main locomotive, reported two days earlier, had not been properly repaired

- the non-standard repair used inappropriate materials, leading to the leaking of oil and the initial fire

- the air brakes were disabled when the fire department shut down the locomotive

- the reset safety control system was not wired properly and didn't set the brakes automatically in the event of engine failure

- the tank cars were prone to puncturing and the Bakken crude oil was highly volatile

- MMA had made operational changes and regulatory oversight was inadequate

- there was no regulatory follow-up to ensure that past safety deficiencies were corrected

- audits of safety management systems were inadequate

- the train was moving too fast for deteriorated track conditions

- the air in the air brakes leaked off, causing the brakes to fail

- the engineer failed to turn off the air brakes before testing the hand brakes

- only seven hand brakes had been set, and 17–26 were needed

- the train was left unattended on a hill, on a main line, and with a malfunctioning main locomotive

- there was no mechanical device on the tracks to prevent the train from rolling away

- the railway employees were poorly trained in securing trains

- MMA had a weak safety culture, and there were gaps between operating instructions and procedures used by crews

- MMA's safety management system, though developed in 2002, had still not been fully implemented by 2013; and

- MMA did not effectively evaluate risks when making operational changes.

The TSB considered whether single-person train operations contributed to the accident, but were unable to conclude that another operator would have made a difference that night. The report also did not address the volatility of oil in its report; although crude is generally not prone to explosion, petroleum from the Bakken field can contain high levels of hydrogen sulphide gas, which is flammable and explosive. Gasification of the crude oil during transportation appears to have led to the catastrophic explosions after the derailment.

The TSB also identified these safety risks, which need to be addressed before another rail disaster occurs: unattended trains, single-person train operations, failure to test petroleum crude oil for volatility, failure to analyze routes on which dangerous goods are transported, absence of emergency response plans, and failure of safety management systems.

Decontamination of the site was expected to take five years. Fortunately, the water table appears to be uncontaminated. Approximately 1,585,000 of 1,770,000 gallons (6 million liters of 6.7 million liters) of crude oil on the train were released. An estimated 26,400 gallons (100,000 liters) of crude oil flowed into Lac Mégantic and Chaudière River along the surface of the ground, through underground filtration, and through the sewer systems. Some new commercial buildings have been erected outside the disaster zone to accommodate residents. But demands by the residents of Lac-Mégantic that rails be rerouted around the town have not been heeded, even though oil shipments were scheduled to resume on the line by 2016.

3

Iroquois Theatre Fire

1903

Illinois, USA

"The screams of the children for their mothers and mothers for their children I shall carry in my memory to my dying day." —Frank Slosson, survivor

The Iroquois Theatre was built in Chicago's central city, on Randolph Street between State and Dearborn, in 1903. The owners, attempting to attract women on trips into the city, chose a location near the Loop shopping district, an area well-patrolled by police. It opened in November 1903, with a capacity of 1,602 on three audience levels: the main floor with about 700 seats, on the same level as the foyer and Grand Stair Hall; the dress circle on the first balcony, with 400 seats; and the gallery on the upper balcony, with 500 seats.

The theatre was advertised as being "absolutely fireproof," but fire safety deficiencies were apparent from the start. Chicago fire ordinances required separate stairways and exits for each balcony, but the Iroquois Theatre was designed with broad stairs from the foyer that climbed to the first and second balconies. *Fireproof Magazine* sent an editor to the theatre, who noted the absence of a stage draft shaft, an opening in the ceiling designed to funnel smoke and flames from a backstage fire through the ceiling like a chimney and draw fresh air into the seating area and smoke out of the building. The editor also noted the prevalence of wood trim everywhere, as well as an inadequate number and placement of exits.

A Chicago Fire Department captain made an unofficial tour days before the theatre opened, and noted the complete lack of sprinklers, alarms, telephones, and water connections to fight a blaze. He pointed out these problems to the theatre's fire warden, who said nothing could be done, because if he brought up the issues with the owners, he would be fired and replaced. The captain made a report to his commanding officer, who said he could do nothing because the theatre already had a fire warden.

The only firefighting equipment in the theatre was six Kilfyre extinguishers. Normally sold to put out house chimney fires, Kilfyre was an early form of dry chemical fire extinguisher, a tube filled with three pounds of white powder consisting mainly of sodium bicarbonate. The instructions told the user to "forcibly hurl" its contents at the base of the flames.

Theatre-goers were well aware of fire hazards in a theatre setting in 1903 because of previous fires with disastrous loss of life. The owners of the Iroquois Theatre claimed that, at capacity, everyone in the theatre could escape through 30 exits within five minutes. But there were many deficiencies in the Iroquois's building and safety systems that would contribute to disaster. Exit doors opened inward, so in a crush of people, the doors could not be opened. There were no exit signs and no emergency lighting. Many exits were covered with draperies which proved to be flammable; other exits were locked. Stairways were blocked during performances to prevent people from moving to more expensive seats without the proper ticket. Exit routes were confusing, and what looked like ornamental doors turned out not to be exits. Iron fire escapes were inadequate and didn't reach the ground.

The smoke doors above the stage were locked shut, so in the event of a fire, smoke would pour into the audience seating area instead of through the ceiling vents. The theatre staff had never practiced a fire drill, and was unfamiliar with emergency exits.

In 1903, fire safety curtains were already in use. When lowered, the fire-resistant curtains protected the audience from flames and smoke. The curtain in the Iroquois had not been regularly tested, and jammed when it was needed most. The curtain even turned out to not be fire resistant. Asbestos was normally woven with metal wire to make an effective barrier between the stage, where many theatre fires broke out, and the audience. But the Iroquois' fire curtain, when tested, proved to be a cheap imitation made of wood pulp and asbestos fibers, too weak to protect the audience from fire, and actually flammable.

On December 30, 1903, only five weeks after the theatre opened, a popular musical, *Mr. Bluebeard*, was performed during a matinee show. The musical had been playing at the Iroquois Theatre since the theatre's opening night. Although previous ticket sales had been disappointing, on this Wednesday afternoon the performance was a sellout. Tickets were sold for every seat in the house, and hundreds more for standing room only areas in the back of the theatre. An estimated 2,100 to 2,200 patrons attended the bargain-priced show, many of them children who were on their Christmas holiday. Because the standing room areas were so crowded, some of those ticket holders moved to the aisles, where they sat and blocked escape routes. Several hundred theatre employees, performers, and crew were also in the building.

At about 3:15 p.m., an arc light shorted out during a dance number; the sparks ignited a muslin curtain about 12 feet (3.6 m) above the stage. A stagehand used a Kilfyre canister to try to put out the flames, which quickly spread above the stage where thousands of square feet (hundreds of square meters) of highly flammable canvas scenery pieces were hanging. Attempts were made to lower the fire curtain, but it snagged on a light reflector and could not be lowered. Because the fire was now raging far above the stage, the remaining Kilfyre canisters served no purpose, as any tossed powder fell harmlessly to the floor.

Actor Eddie Foy, one of the leads and in drag, ran onto the stage and tried to calm the crowd. He later said he had never seen so many women and children in an audience. Foy continued to plead for calm as large pieces of burning scenery crashed to the stage around him.

The main auditorium lights were never turned on, so the space was dimly lit. Tons of burning scenery fell to the stage, destroying the electrical switchboard and turning out all the lights in the theatre.

Audience members from all levels of the theatre were trying to flee the building by this point. Some of them found the fire exits behind draperies, but they didn't know how to operate the levers which fastened them closed. Many had trouble finding exits and were killed in dead-end passages or at the decorative doors that weren't really doors. About 200 people died in one of the passageways that led nowhere. Teenage ushers, eager to flee the inferno, left the emergency exits and iron gates on the stairways locked.

At least 125 people died on the fire escapes on the building exterior, which were still unfinished. The steps and ladders were icy, and people found themselves trapped by smoke and flames. Many jumped or fell to their deaths as the railings collapsed. Some jumpers survived when they landed on top of other bodies, which broke their fall.

Students in the neighboring Northwestern University building erected a makeshift bridge with ladders and boards, reportedly saving 12 people.

The stairway design proved disastrous in the panic. As gallery patrons descended the stairs, they encountered the crowd from the balcony level, already jammed on the stairs. Those who managed to descend to the main floor ran into the locked iron gates at the bottom of the stairs. The highest death toll was at the base of these stairways, where hundreds were trampled or suffocated by the crush of people.

The cast and crew rushed to escape. When the rear door was opened to the alley, an icy wind whipped into the theatre, feeding the flames. Some escaped through coal chutes. Many became trapped against the west stage door, which opened inward. A passing railroad agent saw the crowd pressed against the doors and used his tools, which he carried with him everywhere, to unfasten the hinges and let the people escape. A large set of double doors, used to get scenery in and out of the building, was opened; another blast of cold air rushed into the theatre and created a fireball. Because the ceiling vents were locked shut, the fireball passed under the partly-lowered fire curtain and passed over the heads of the people still trapped in their main level seats and incinerated anything flammable in the two balcony areas. Many people burned to death.

One stagehand escaped and ran to a nearby fire station for help. The responding firefighters sounded another alarm to bring more men and equipment to the scene. Initially, firefighters focused on the people on the fire escapes, but the alley was narrow and full of smoke, so ladders and nets proved useless. A Chicago police officer on patrol saw people running from the building in a panic; he called in from a police box, and soon officers were converging on the theatre from all over the city.

Firefighters were able to bring the fire under control in 15 minutes. First responders found corpses piled ten high around the windows and doors. The death toll was about 602, including 27 injured victims who died afterward. Another 250 were injured. It was the deadliest single-building fire in American history.

Only five of the 300 actors and crew died. Aerialist Nellie Reed, whose role in the play was to fly on wires over the audience dressed as a fairy and shower the audience with carnations, was trapped high above the stage, hanging on her wires. She eventually fell to the stage and died of burns and injuries three days later.

Survivors recounted stories of teenage ushers who closed doors and refused to let people pass, to get them to go back to their seats. They also said the building's windows were covered in steel plates on the outside which were bolted shut. Most of the dead had been sitting in the two balcony levels.

By the next day, theaters across the country were eliminating standing room areas. Theaters were closed in many cities for retrofitting to conform to stricter fire safety standards, including clearly marked exits and outward-opening doors. Chicago's mayor ordered all theaters closed for six weeks for inspection and upgrades. The fire prompted many large-occupancy buildings to install panic bars, allowing fleeing people to push locked doors open in an emergency. But it would take another fire disaster, this time in a school full of children, before outward-swinging doors would be required across the country.

Allegations were made that fire inspectors had been bribed with free theatre tickets to turn their heads from code violations. Public outrage led to criminal charges against numerous people, including the mayor, but most charges were dismissed on technicalities, and the only conviction was for grave robbing by a tavern owner whose saloon was used as a temporary morgue.

The Iroquois Theatre, which hadn't suffered major damage, would be reconstructed and reopened as the Colonial Theater within a year. The building was subsequently demolished in 1926 and the Oriental Theater was built on the site.

4

Al-Aaimmah Bridge Stampede

2005

Iraq

*"[Women, children, and the elderly] were crying,
shouting out 'please rescue me', but there was no way to
help them."* —Hadi Shakir, street trader

The Al-Aaimmah bridge over the Tigris River in
Baghdad, Iraq, connects Adhamiya, the majority Sunni Arab
area on the east side, with Kadhimiya, the Shia area on the
west bank. On August 31, 2005, approximately one million
pilgrims were heading for the Al Kadhimiya Mosque on the
west side of the river for a religious festival. Each year, Shiite
followers commemorate the martyrdom of Imam Moussa al-
Khadhem, a prominent Shiite who is buried there. Earlier
that day, a mortar attack targeted the crowd at the Shi'ite
shrine; seven had been killed and dozens wounded. A Sunni
insurgent group linked with Al-Qaeda, Jaysh al-Taifa al-
Mansoura (Army of the Victorious Sect), claimed
responsibility. The crowd was fearful of another attack.

Near the mosque, rumors of an imminent suicide bomb
attack spread, and the crowd panicked. Interior Minister
Bayan Baqir Solagh later said that one person "pointed a
finger at another person saying that he was carrying
explosives...and that led to the panic."

The panicked crowd fled the area and headed for the
bridge, at which barricades and security searches added to
the congestion. Despite the bridge being closed with gates

across both ends, the western gates were opened and the pilgrims swarmed onto the bridge. The eastern gate remained closed, however (it opened inward), and many suffocated from the crush of people. The iron railings on the bridge gave way, and many people went over the side of the bridge, falling 30 feet (9 m) into the Tigris. The death toll was 953, with 810 injured; many of them were elderly, women, and children. Some were crushed or trampled; others drowned in the river.

The stampede was mostly ignored by the American media; two days earlier, Hurricane Katrina had struck New Orleans and the Gulf Coast, and that story was dominating the news in the U.S. On the day of the stampede, American viewers were instead watching live video feeds of helicopter rescues from rooftops in New Orleans as well as the unfolding humanitarian disaster at the Superdome.

5

Cavalese Cable Car Disaster

1998

Italy

"This is a very serious accident which should not have happened." —Lamberto Dini, Italian Foreign Minister

"There's no justice in the world." —John Eaves, a lawyer representing the families of the seven German victims

On February 3, 1998, a U.S. Marine Corps EA-6B Prowler electronic warfare aircraft was on a low-altitude training mission over the Italian Alps. At 14:13 local time, while flying at 540 mph (870 kph), the aircraft struck and severed the cables supporting an aerial tramway gondola between Cavalese and the summit of Mount Cermis, Italy. Twenty people (19 passengers and the cable car operator) perished when the car plunged 260 feet (80 m) to the ground. The aircraft, despite wing and tail damage, was able to return to NATO's Aviano Air Base, its home base.

When the Prowler severed the cable, it was flying just under its maximum speed of 550 mph (885 kph), and had veered from the route authorized by the Italian government.

The crew had been deployed to Aviano to train for missions over Bosnia. Italian prosecutors wanted the four Marines involved in the disaster to be tried in Italy, but an Italian court agreed that NATO treaties gave U.S. military courts jurisdiction in the case.

The official Marine Corps report from March 10, 1998, determined that the aircraft was flying too fast and too low, and they had put themselves and others at great risk. The squadron had been deployed at Aviano after the Italian government issued new rules establishing the 2,000 foot (610 m) minimum. On January 24, the crew had received a formal warning for flying too low during a training mission. All pilots had received a copy of these new rules, but the letter was later found unopened in the cockpit, along with updated maps showing cables, when the plane landed at Aviano after the accident. On the morning of the flight, the radar altimeter checked out fine by maintenance crews, before and after the flight. The report recommended disciplinary measures be taken against the crew and that the U.S. had to bear the full blame for the disaster. It also recommended monetary compensation for the victims' families. This report was redacted, classified, and kept secret until a copy was legally obtained by *La Stampa*, an Italian newspaper, in 2011.

The crew had received American military charts to plan their route that day; the maps did not show the cables. The U.S. military's policy was not to rely on maps made in foreign countries. Italian maps provided to the Marine Corps clearly showed the cable route.

Just before the disaster, witnesses reported that the plane roared through the valley, skimming just above houses, lakes, and roads, frightening the local residents. After a Prowler crashed on a training flight in Arizona in 1996, the Pentagon ordered a 1,000 feet (310 m) minimum flight path for the aircraft, considerably higher than the Cavalese cable. A power line had been cut by a low-flying Italian military jet in the same area in 1996, resulting in complaints by local officials.

All four men on the plane were charged, but Captain Richard J. Ashby, the pilot, and Captain Joseph Schweitzer, the navigator, were the only two to stand trial. They were charged with 20 counts of involuntary manslaughter and negligent homicide. During the trial, at Camp Lejeune in North Carolina, it was determined that the aircraft was flying faster and lower than military regulations allowed; the minimum flying height restriction at the time was 2,000 feet (610 m), although the pilot claimed he thought it was 1,000 feet (305 m). The cable was cut at a height of 360 feet (110 m). He also claimed that he was unaware of the speed restrictions, that the height-measuring equipment on the plane had malfunctioned, and that the maps on board did not show the cables. The eight-member jury accepted the defense argument that the accident was caused by an optical illusion, making the cable appear further away than it really was. Ashby was acquitted by the jury in March 1999, and the charges against Schweitzer were then dropped. The Italians expressed outrage.

Shortly thereafter, the existence of a videotape of the flight came to the attention of military investigators. The videotape had been removed by the crew after the plane landed and had been destroyed. Schweitzer later claimed he feared the Italian media would use footage of him smiling into the camera coupled with video of the smashed gondola and blood-stained snow. In a second trial, the two were court-martialed for obstruction of justice and conduct unbecoming an officer and a gentleman. They were found guilty in May 1999. Both were dismissed from the Marine Corps, and the pilot was given a six-month prison term. He was released after four-and-a-half months for good behavior. Schweitzer confessed in 2012 that the videotape had been burned upon their return to base because it would reveal the truth about the crew's negligence.

The Italian government provided victims' families with $65,000 in February 1999; this amount was reimbursed by the U.S. government. In December 1999, a compensation package of $1.9 million per victim was approved by the Italian legislature. The U.S. paid 75% of that amount, in accordance with NATO treaties. Relations between the two countries were strained because of the disaster and its handling by the American military.

This was not the first disaster on the Cavalese cable car. On March 9, 1976, the supporting cable snapped, and 43 people, 15 of them children, perished in the worst cable car accident in history.

6

SL-1 Meltdown

1961

Idaho, USA

"Victim of nuclear accident. Body is contaminated with long-life radio-active isotopes. Under no circumstances will the body be moved from this location without prior approval of the Atomic Energy Commission in consultation with this headquarters." —permanent records of Richard L. McKinley grave at Arlington National Cemetery

By 1955, the U.S. Army decided that they needed nuclear reactors that could operate in remote northern regions. These nuclear power plants would replace diesel generators and boilers, to provide electricity and heating at radar stations in the Arctic and along the DEW Line (Distant Early Warning Line, a system of radar installations across far northern North America whose job it was to detect incoming Soviet bombers).

The prototype reactor was constructed in 1957–1958 at the Nuclear Reactor Testing Station (NRTS), about 40 miles (64 km) west of Idaho Falls, Idaho. It became operational in 1958 and was dubbed the SL-1, or Stationary Low-Power Reactor Number One. The reactor was housed in a cylindrical steel building sheathed in quarter-inch (6 mm) plate steel, which accessed through ordinary doors. There was no containment shell around the building because of the remoteness of the site; a similar reactor in a more populated area in the U.S. would have had a pressure containment system such as is used at most nuclear reactor facilities today.

On January 3, 1961, after being shut down for eleven days over the holidays for maintenance, the three-man team was preparing for a restart of the reactor. Maintenance procedures required that the main control rod be manually withdrawn four inches (10 cm) to reconnect it to the automated drive mechanism. At 9:01 p.m., the rod was suddenly withdrawn 26 inches (66 cm), causing the reactor to go critical, and resulting in a meltdown and steam explosion. The fuel and water surrounding the fuel was vaporized in the extreme heat; this vaporization occurred within 7.5 milliseconds. In a reactor designed for a 3 megawatt power output, power was momentarily generated at a level of nearly 20 gigawatts in just four milliseconds, more than 6,000 times the reactor's safe operating limit.

The blast caused the coolant water to shoot upward inside the reactor, resulting in a pressure wave that propelled the control rods, shield plugs, and the entire 26,000-pound (12,000-kg) reactor vessel nine feet into the air, where it struck the ceiling and sprayed steam and water out of the top of the reactor. The vessel then settled back into its normal position.

Three operators were in the reactor building at the time: Army Specialists John A. Byrnes, 27, and Richard Leroy McKinley, 22; and Navy Seabee Construction Electrician First Class (CE1) Richard C. Legg, 26. Disaster reconstructionists later determined that Byrnes, the reactor operator, had lifted the rod, leading to the explosion. Standing on top of the reactor was Legg, the shift supervisor. McKinley was a trainee, standing nearby. There was no one else at the site.

Heat sensors in the building set off an alarm at 9:01 p.m. at the fire station and security headquarters at the central test site facility. Six firemen arrived nine minutes later; they expected it to be a false alarm, as false alarms had sounded twice earlier that day. They noticed nothing unusual at first, but noted a radiation warning light in the facility and withdrew. At 9:17, a health physicist arrived, and with one of the firemen, attempted to climb the stairs into the building, but their equipment indicated high radiation, and they too retreated. Shortly thereafter, another team arrived, and ascended the stairs, discovering damage in the reactor room. They quickly retreated; radiation meters indicated high-level radiation had filled the complex.

About 10:30 p.m., another team entered the building and found two mutilated men; Byrnes was dead, but McKinley was moaning and moving slightly. Rescuers were allowed only one entry into the building for a maximum of one minute. McKinley, still breathing, was removed on a stretcher, but did not regain consciousness and died at about 11:00 of a head injury.

At 10:38, the rescue team discovered Legg's body. The explosion had sent one of the shield plugs upward, impaling Legg, who was standing on top of the reactor, pinning him to the ceiling. With all three occupants of the building accounted for, the recovery operation slowed down to reduce the team's exposure to radiation. On January 4, Byrnes' body was recovered, and on January 9, the team managed to pull Legg's body from the ceiling. The three bodies were buried in lead-lined caskets, sealed in concrete, and placed in metal vaults with concrete covers. Some highly radioactive body parts, such as the hands, were considered radioactive waste and removed from the bodies, and were then buried in the desert. McKinley was laid to rest at Arlington National Cemetery.

But why had the control rod been removed past the point that operators knew would cause a meltdown? Maintenance logs do not reveal what the technicians were doing at the time, and all witnesses are dead. A two-year investigation ensued. Four theories were proposed: sabotage or suicide, murder-suicide, inadvertent withdrawal of the rod, and intentionally "exercising" the rod so that it moved more freely. Experiments revealed the most likely explanation, based on the locations of the bodies and other evidence: the 84-pound (38-kg) rod had become stuck (which had happened before), and, in trying to free it, Byrnes accidentally broke the rod loose and withdrew it. The result was a meltdown, explosion, and radiation release, the only such incident in American history which resulted in immediate deaths. The release of radioactive products into the atmosphere was not considered significant because of the remoteness of the location, and the fact that the building had contained most of the radioactivity.

There was, however, evidence indicating that Byrnes was having marital problems, or even believed his wife was having an affair with one of the other men present, and may have triggered the explosion intentionally. The official government report ignored this evidence.

The damage inside the reactor was caused by hydraulic shock, also called a water hammer, as the coolant water was propelled upwards. The shock wave also killed the three operators and released radioactive isotopes into the atmosphere. The analysis of the incident led to a recommendation that reactors be filled to the top with water, to minimize the risk of water hammer damage. The extra water also provides protection from radioactive contamination for those above the vessel.

This nuclear meltdown led to the abandonment of the design used in the SL-1 reactor, so that the total removal of one rod cannot lead to a power surge that can cause a similar disaster. Procedures for operating nuclear reactors became considerably more detailed. After the Army evaluated its program, they pursued the use of Mobile Low-Power Reactors (ML-1), which began operation in 1963. But by 1965 the development program was halted due to the financial pressures of the Vietnam War. The last of the reactors were shut down by 1977.

The SL-1 site was cleared over 18 months in 1961 and 1962. Most of the contaminated debris was buried at a specially-built site 1,600 feet (500 m) from the reactor site, instead of the Radioactive Waste Management Complex 16 miles (26 km) away, to minimize the radioactive threat from moving it. Remedial action to clean the site was still taking place as recently as the year 2000. The accident and its cleanup eventually resulted in the exposure of 790 people to harmful levels of radiation.

January 4, 1961: Health physicists check Highway 20 for contamination on the morning after the SL-1 accident.

7

Basra Mass Grain Poisoning

1971–72

Iraq

With a serious ongoing drought impacting the harvest in Iraq in 1969 and 1970, the country's second in command, Saddam Hussein, decided to import seed grain for the planting season in late 1971. The grain, purchased from Mexico and the United States, was coated in methylmercury; mercury functions as a fungicide when sprayed onto seed grain. The grain was not intended for human consumption, and was dyed a pink-orange hue.

The health risks of mercury had been known for some time; it was banned in Sweden in 1966 and in the U.K. in 1971. Mercury poisoning incidents had taken place in Iraq in 1956 (approximately 200 cases with 70 deaths) and 1960 (1,000 cases with 200 deaths). After the 1960 poisoning, it was recommended that toxic grains be dyed for easy identification. Saddam Hussein was working in the Department of Agriculture during the 1960 event.

In 1971, 73,201 tons (66,407 metric tons) of wheat grain and 22,262 tons (20,196 metric tons) of barley with a pink-orange dye applied was shipped to Iraq and distributed to rural areas. The grain was distributed too late in the season to be planted, so many farmers ingested the grain instead. The grain made its way into the food chain as an ingredient in homemade bread, in meat obtained from animals (mainly sheep) that were fed the tainted grain, from eating birds that had consumed the grain, and from fish caught in water into which the tainted grain had been dumped. Ground seed dust was also inhaled by many people in rural areas that had received the grain.

The grain sacks had warnings printed in English and Spanish and included black-and-white skull and crossbones warnings; but this meant nothing to Iraqis. The dye was easily removed by washing, which gave recipients a false sense that any contaminants had been removed, but the mercury remained coated on the grain. Animals fed the grain appeared to be fine because of the long latent period for mercury poisoning. To receive the initial shipment of grain, farmers were required to certify with a signature or thumbprint that they understood that the grain had been poisoned, but many remained unaware of the danger or chose to ignore it. Many reports surfaced later that indicated this information was not provided by distributors.

The effects of mercury poisoning took 16–38 days to show as symptoms. Paresthesia (numbness of skin), ataxia (lack of muscle movement coordination and loss of balance), and vision loss began to appear. The worst cases resulted in death from central nervous system failure.

The first case of alkylmercury poisoning appeared at the Kirkuk hospital on December 21, 1971. Large numbers of symptomatic patients soon arrived, and the hospital warned the Iraqi government on December 26. In January 1972, the Iraqi government warned citizens about the poison grain, and the army ordered the disposal of the grain and threatened the death penalty to anyone selling the tainted grain. Farmers dumped their supplies of grain, which entered the main bodies of water, further tainting the food supply. The Iraqi government responded by issuing a news blackout, and essentially stopped releasing information to the general population.

*A sack of the poisoned grain. The labeling is in Spanish;
the grain is distinctively orange-pink in color.*

All told, 6,530 patients were admitted to hospitals with
mercury poisoning symptoms; 459 deaths were officially
reported. This was the largest death toll from poisoning at
the time. The official toll is almost certainly an
underestimate because of the Middle Eastern custom that a
person dies at home; deaths at home were not reported in
the official tally. Some Iraqi doctors believe the real toll was

43

10 times the official number. The outbreak was over by the end of March.

A 1974 meeting of the Food and Agriculture Organization (FAO) and World Health Organization (WHO) recommended changes to prevent a future outbreak, including proper package labeling in the local language and warning signs that would be understood by the local populace.

8

Centralia Underground Coal Fire

1962–ca. 2265

Pennsylvania, USA

"Warning — Danger. Underground Mine Fire. Walking or Driving in this Area Could Result in Serious Injury or Death. Dangerous Gases are Present. Ground is Prone to Sudden Collapse" —sign posted by the Pennsylvania Department of Environmental Protection

Abandoned coal mines under the Pennsylvania town of Centralia are the scene of an ongoing man-made ecological disaster. Since at least May 27, 1962, a coal seam fire has been burning in an area as much as 300 feet (91 m) deep, eight miles (12.9 km) long, and in an area of 3,700 acres (1,500 hectares). The fire continues to this day, and could burn for another 250 years.

In early 1962, Centralia had eight illegal dumps operating around the town. To stop illegal dumping, the town opened a new landfill. A 50-foot (15-m) deep old strip mine was dug out into a 300-foot (91-m) by 75-foot (23-m) pit. In 1956, Pennsylvania had enacted regulations for using strip mines for landfills because they were known to cause destructive mine fires. During an inspection of the Centralia landfill, the inspector noticed holes in the walls and floor of the pit, indicating that mine shafts had been cut through. He informed a Centralia councilman that the pit was required to be filled with noncombustible material. The council decided to clear the dump and hired five members of the volunteer fire department to clean up the landfill, despite a state law

45

that prohibited dump fires.

On May 27, 1962, a fire was ignited in the dump, which the fire department extinguished. Flames flared up twice more within a week, so a bulldozer was brought in to stir up the burning waste so the fire department could douse the burning lower layers of garbage. The excavation revealed a hole in the pit 15 feet (4.6 m) wide and several feet high that had been concealed by garbage and had not been filled with noncombustible material; this was most likely the gateway to the mine fire. Locals complained about the smell of smoldering trash and coal on July 2, even as the council still allowed trash to be dumped into the pit.

Smoke was soon seen rising from fissures in the pit wall. Testing indicated that carbon monoxide was seeping out of the ground, an indication that a coal seam was burning. The council, attempting to conceal the truth of the matter, alerted the Lehigh Valley Coal Company to the fire, stating that the fire was "of unknown origin...during a period of unusually hot weather."

The Lehigh Valley Coal Company had also fought a fire in another mine for more than 80 years, from 1859 to the 1940s, at a cost of $2 million.

By August, lethal levels of carbon monoxide were measured, and all area mines were closed by state inspectors.

Meager attempts were made over the next several months to excavate the seam that was burning, but the attempts were poorly planned and funded, and soon funding was cut off altogether. Another attempt was made to smother the fire with a water-and-crushed-rock mixture, but a harsh winter which froze the water supply hastened the failure of that attempt.

In April, it was discovered that the fire had spread east at least 700 feet (210 m), and steam started to curl up from fissures in the ground. The state made plans to smother the fire in 1963, but the project was delayed until the new fiscal year began on July 1, 1963, and then cancelled altogether before it had begun.

The fire continued to burn unchecked. In 1979, the local population began to understand the size of the problem. Mayor John Coddington, the owner of a gas station, lowered a dipstick into one of his underground gas tanks and it came out hot. He lowered a thermometer into the tank and found the temperature inside the tank was 172°F (77.8°C).

By 1980, several people were reporting health issues from carbon monoxide, carbon dioxide, and low levels of oxygen. In 1981, a 12-year-old fell into a 4-foot (1.2-m) wide sinkhole that suddenly opened under his feet in his backyard; the hole was 150 feet (46 m) deep. He clung to a tree root until he was pulled out of the sinkhole. A lethal level of carbon monoxide was measured in the steam plume emanating from the sinkhole. These events led to greater statewide attention to the problem. But by this point the state and federal government had given up trying to put out the fire.

Congress authorized more than $42 million for relocation efforts for Centralia. In 1992, Governor Bob Casey invoked eminent domain on all properties in the borough and condemned all of the buildings. The U.S. Postal Service revoked Centralia's ZIP code in 2002. All but a handful of residents accepted buyout offers and moved to neighboring communities. The ongoing coal fire has resulted in Centralia being practically abandoned. The town's population of 2,761 in 1980 had fallen to 7 in 2013. Most of the buildings have been leveled. A few families decided to stay. Officials agreed to allow the last seven residents to live out their lives in the town; after their deaths, their properties will be taken through eminent domain. Just to the south, the town of Byrnesville was completely abandoned and leveled in 1996.

In this photo dated Feb. 14, 1981, Todd Domboski looks over a barricade at the hole he fell through just hours before this photo was taken in Centralia, Pennsylvania. The hole was caused by a mine fire that had been burning beneath the town since 1962, and continues to burn today.

Today, the Centralia area has become somewhat of a tourist destination. Smoke can be seen seeping up from the ground along the empty streets of the town. A portion of Pennsylvania Route 61 has been destroyed and abandoned; in the woods along the road, trees have been baked to death. Long cracks have torn the highway apart; heat, steam, and carbon dioxide seep from the fissures. A new route bypasses the destroyed section near where Byrnesville once was located.

Amazingly, Centralia is not the longest burning coal vein fire. A coal mine fire near Glenwood Springs, Colorado, has been burning since 1910. Scientists estimate that Australia's Burning Mountain has been burning for 6,000 years.

9

Sultana Steamboat Explosion

1865

Tennessee, USA

". . . one of the boilers exploded and the greater part of that human load was blown into the river, while sound asleep—some to awake in the cold water and some in eternity. Those that were not blown off at the time of the explosion were soon compelled to jump into the river so as to escape burning to death, for the boat quickly caught fire and burned to the water's edge." —Samuel H. Raudebaugh, excerpted from *"Loss of the Sultana and Reminiscences of Survivors"* by Rev. Chester D. Berry, 1892

The SS *Sultana* was a side-wheel steamboat that carried goods and passengers up and down the Mississippi River. Built in 1863, the 260-foot (79-m) long boat with four decks and a crew of 85 had a carrying capacity of 376 passengers. It was built to service the lower Mississippi River cotton trade. The *Sultana* frequently carried troops for the U.S. government between St. Louis and New Orleans in the midst of the American Civil War.

The *Sultana* left St. Louis on April 13, 1865 on her regular run to New Orleans. While docked in Cairo, Illinois, on the morning of April 15, word reached the crew that President Abraham Lincoln had been shot the night before in Ford's Theater. Captain J. Cass Mason headed south to spread the news; telegraphic communication had been severely disrupted in the south because of the war, which had officially ended just six days earlier.

Thousands of prisoners held in Confederate prisoner-of-war camps such as Cahaba (Selma, Alabama) and Andersonville, Georgia, had been brought to a parole camp near Vicksburg, Mississippi, awaiting their release. When the *Sultana* reached Vicksburg, the chief quartermaster at Vicksburg, Lt. Col. Reuben Hatch, approached Captain Mason with a deal. The U.S. Government was offering to pay $5 per enlisted man and $10 per officer to take the former prisoners back to the north. The two men agreed on a plan for the *Sultana* to take on a load of 1,400 prisoners, with Lt. Col. Hatch receiving a share of the funds as a kickback. The *Sultana* continued on to New Orleans, spreading the word of Lincoln's assassination, while the prisoners were prepared for transfer.

On April 21, the *Sultana* left New Orleans. On board were 75 to 100 cabin passengers, deck passengers, and some livestock. An hour south of Vicksburg, one of the steamboat's boilers sprung a leak. The boat made it to Vicksburg to receive repairs and pick up the prisoners.

A mechanic, R. G. Taylor, repaired the boiler, one of four on the boat, while the prisoners were moved from the parole camp and brought aboard. The mechanic wanted to replace a section of ruptured seam, but Captain Mason knew that would take several days, and therefore the prisoners would be transferred to other boats and he would lose his commission. Mason and chief engineer Nathan Wintringer ordered the mechanic, over Taylor's objections, to make temporary repairs by riveting a thin piece of new boiler plate over the bulging seam. The steamboat was ready to sail in just one day.

Instead of the 1,400 prisoners that Hatch had promised Mason, Capt. George Williams, the Union officer in charge of the operation, placed every man at the parole camp on the *Sultana*. When the steamboat sailed from Vicksburg on the night of April 24, approximately 2,100 paroled prisoners were crowded on the decks, on a boat with a capacity of 376. The weight of the men caused the decks to sag; they were reinforced with heavy wooden beams.

The Mississippi River was experiencing one of the worst spring flooding seasons ever recorded. The river spread over its banks three miles wide in places. Trees along the river bank were almost completely inundated; only their tops stuck out of the raging floodwaters. The *Sultana* pushed its boilers to fight the torrent of water and proceeded upstream.

The *Sultana* reached Memphis, Tennessee, about 7:00 p.m., and 120 tons of sugar was unloaded. Around midnight, the steamboat went a short distance upriver to replenish its coal supply, and then continued upstream again.

At about 2:00 a.m., on April 27, 1865, just seven miles north of Memphis, near Paddy's Hen and Chicken Islands, one of the boilers suddenly exploded, triggering further explosions in two other boilers. Passengers were sprayed with red-hot shrapnel, boiling water, and burning coal and embers. Much of the boat was immediately destroyed, and passengers were flung from the deck into the raging current. In the forward portion of the ship, the upper decks collapsed into the now-exposed furnace boxes, igniting what remained of the ship into a flaming inferno.

The steamboat had only one lifeboat and few life preservers. The paroled prisoners who survived the blast jumped overboard to save themselves. Most of them were already in poor physical condition due to malnutrition, exposure, and illness from the appalling conditions in Southern prisoner-of-war camps. The soldiers were as young as 14, and many of them drowned in the swiftly-moving current.

About an hour after the explosion, the steamer *Bostona II*, heading downriver on her maiden voyage, arrived at the scene, and began taking on dozens of survivors. At the same time, dozens of survivors were floating past the docks in Memphis, crying out for help. Other vessels then joined in the search for other survivors. Many of those who leapt into the water to save themselves died of drowning or hypothermia; the river was filled with floodwater from the melted snowpack to the north. Some survivors clung to treetops above the floodwaters. Bodies were found downstream for months, as far south as Vicksburg. Captain Mason and the rest of his officers were among those killed.

What was left of the *Sultana* drifted six miles downstream and finally sank on the west bank of the Mississippi, seven hours after the explosion, east of Marion, Arkansas.

Approximately 1,800 of the *Sultana's* 2,427 passengers died in the worst maritime disaster in American history. However, about 700 people had survived the disaster. Many of them suffered from burns, and as many as 200 died later from their injuries or from exposure. Many of the dead were buried at Memphis National Cemetery; many others were never recovered.

Secretary of War Edwin Stanton created a board of inquiry on April 30, 1865. The explosion was blamed on the crew exceeding the maximum steam pressure while attempting to move upstream against the floodwaters, compounded by low water levels in the boilers. The boat was also severely crowded and therefore top heavy, causing it to noticeably list from side to side as it traveled around the many bends of the Mississippi River. The four boilers were connected and mounted side by side, so when the ship listed, low water levels in the boilers would cause water to pour from the highest boiler into the others. With the boiler fires continuing to burn, the partially empty boiler would overheat; when water poured back in as the boat listed the other way, the water would flash to steam instantly and create pressure surges. The official inquiry determined that the explosion was also partially caused by the faulty, temporary repair made to the boiler.

No one was ever held accountable for the disaster. The military refused to try Capt. Williams, who had placed the men on board. Col. Hatch promptly quit the service and was no longer accountable to a military court, despite having conspired to overcrowd the steamboat.

In 1888, Robert Louden, a former Confederate agent, reportedly made a deathbed confession that he had sabotaged the *Sultana* with a coal torpedo. However, this claim is generally disregarded as the official explanation fits the available facts.

The *Sultana* disaster received little attention at the time. The Civil War had just ended, Lincoln had been murdered, and his assassin, John Wilkes Booth, had just been killed the day before the *Sultana* explosion. Americans were weary of hearing about death and destruction.

The disaster resulted in new safety regulations and regular steamboat inspections.

An archaeological expedition in 1982 reportedly discovered the remains of the *Sultana* 32 feet (10 m) under a soybean field on the Arkansas side of the river about four miles (6 km) upstream from Memphis. Burned wooden decking was discovered at the site. The remains of the steamboat are now on dry land because of the ever-changing course of the Mississippi's riverbed, which is currently about

2 miles (3 km) east of where the riverbed was in 1865. Most artifacts remain in their original resting place.

On April 26, 1865, the USS Sultana stopped at Helena, Arkansas, where T.W. Bankes photographed the overcrowded vessel.

10

Door to Hell Fire

1971–present

USSR/Turkmenistan

"[The Door to Hell] takes your breath away. You immediately think of your sins and feel like praying." — Gozel Yazkulieva, local resident

Not all disasters result in the loss of human life, but can wreak havoc with humans in the long term.

Soviet engineers identified an area in the Karakum Desert in Turkmenistan as a substantial oil field in 1971. A drilling rig was constructed to extract the rich deposit of natural gas near the town of Derweze (population about 350). Before long, the drilling punctured a massive cavern filled with natural gas. The ground collapsed and formed a 20-foot (6-m) crater 66 feet (20 m) deep. The drilling rig disappeared into the crater, although no lives were lost.

Soviet engineers examined the crater and feared further releases of poisonous gas, which would pose a danger to the local population. The decision was made to burn off the natural gas, so it was lit on fire. It was believed that the fire would burn out in a few weeks. That was 1971; it is still burning today.

Locals refer to the gas field as "The Door to Hell" due to the fire and the pungent sulfurous fumes that pervade the area. Flames and extreme heat emanate from the crater. The remote site is not fenced off and visitors can walk right up to it and stand on the edge of the crater, even though the sandy soil is unstable.

Gurbanguly Berdimuhamedow, the President of Turkmenistan, in the hopes of expanding the country's natural gas exports, in 2010 ordered the hole closed, but no action was taken. Perhaps this is because the burning crater is becoming a destination for foreign tourists, and Turkmenistan desperately needs tourists and their money. Tourism officials are now marketing the Door to Hell to ecotourists and extreme sports enthusiasts. In fact, in 2013, National Geographic partially funded an expedition by George Kourounis to descend to the crater floor to collect biological specimens; the adventure was telecast on the National Geographic Channel in 2014.

In 2013, President Berdimuhamedow designated the site and the surrounding 220,000 acres (90,000 hectares) as a nature reserve. He is apparently convinced now that the ongoing environmental disaster has its silver lining.

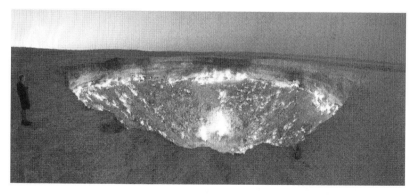

Photo by Tormod Sandtorv

11

Triangle Shirtwaist Factory Fire

1911

New York, USA

"Horrified and helpless, the crowds — I among them — looked up at the burning building, saw girl after girl appear at the reddened windows, pause for a terrified moment, and then leap to the pavement below, to land as mangled, bloody pulp." —Louis Waldman, witness

In 1911, the Triangle Shirtwaist Company occupied the top three floors of the 10-story Asch Building at Greene Street and Washington Place in Manhattan. The company, owned by Max Blanck and Isaac Harris, produced women's blouses, which at the time were also known as "shirtwaists." It was the largest manufacturer of blouses in the country. About 500 workers were employed there; most were young immigrant women. They toiled there for nine hours on weekdays and seven hours on Saturday, for between $7 and $12 per week (a 2014 equivalent of $3.20 to $5.50 per hour).

Workers had organized a strike in 1909 to bring attention to hazardous working conditions, including overcrowding, poor ventilation, and dangerous machinery. A general strike was called in the city in the fall of 1909, and 20,000 workers walked off the job in the first large-scale strike by women workers in American history. A settlement was reached to give workers a slight wage increase, but demands by the union for improved fire safety were not addressed.

Near the end of the Saturday shift on March 25, 1911, a small fire broke out in a scrap bin under a cutting table in a corner of the eighth floor. The wooden scrap bin had not been emptied for about two months, and contained hundreds of pounds of flammable material. The fire marshal later concluded that a discarded match or cigarette most likely ignited the blaze. Workers initially tried to douse the fire using pails of water, as they had done numerous times in the past.

Smoking was banned in the factory, but workers were known to sneak cigarette breaks regularly. Because of this, the owners had locked the stairwells and exits to prevent unauthorized breaks, and to prevent workers from stealing material and supplies.

The first fire alarm was called in by a passerby, who noticed smoke coming from an eighth-floor window. An employee on the eighth floor telephoned the tenth floor to warn them of the fire, but there was no way to contact the ninth floor, and there was no fire alarm to be sounded. There was no formal evacuation plan. The ninth floor had a number of exits: two freight elevators, a fire escape, and two stairways. Fire was already blocking one of the stairways by the time the fire reached the floor and occupants were alerted to the blaze, and the foreman, who had the only keys to the other stairway, quickly escaped via one of the other routes. Some ninth-floor occupants retreated to the roof, while others escaped via the elevators, which continued to function. Elevator operators continued to evacuate people to the ground floor until the elevator car rails buckled due to the heat. Within minutes, the only viable escape route was the fire escape, which had been approved by the city of New York instead of the required third stairway. The fire escape was poorly anchored and too flimsy to hold that much weight, and it soon collapsed, dumping about 20 people almost 100 feet (30 m) to their deaths. Regardless, it would have taken three hours to evacuate everyone on the fire escape. Others pried open the elevator doors and jumped down the shaft to escape the flames.

Horrified and helpless bystanders gathered on the street below and watched 62 people leap or fall to their death on the sidewalk below. Falling workers with their clothing on fire plunged through the glass of sidewalk windows, starting a fire in the basement of the building. Falling bodies, as well as the mass of bodies already on the ground, prevented firefighters from effectively fighting the blaze. Besides, their longest ladders would only reach the sixth floor.

The death toll at the Triangle Shirtwaist Factory fire was 146, 123 of them women. Nearly 100 people fell to their deaths. Seventy-one were injured. Other victims died from fire or smoke inhalation. The two youngest workers killed were 14 years old. Six victims remained unidentified until 2011.

Both owners were in the building at the time of the fire, as were their children. They survived the fire by escaping to the roof. The owners were indicted on charges of first- and second-degree manslaughter. At the trial, the defense successfully argued that witness statements were staged and the owners were unaware the doors were locked that day (although it was their policy to be locked during work hours). The jury acquitted both men. In a subsequent civil lawsuit in 1913, the plaintiffs were awarded $75 per victim; however, the insurance company had paid the owners $60,000 more than their reported losses, equating to about $400 per victim, leaving a profit for the owners. In 1913, Blanck was arrested and fined $20 for locking the door to his factory yet again.

The consequences and legacy of one of America's deadliest industrial disasters quickly took form. Socialist and union activists used the fire to get factory workers to organize. The disaster helped spur the growth of the International Ladies' Garment Workers' Union, which pushed for improved conditions for workers. New York City established a Committee on Public Safety, to identify problems and lobby for new legislation to improve working conditions. The State of New York also created the Factory Investigating Commission to propose legislation to reduce the hazards of unsafe working conditions, including fire, sanitation, and public health; sixty-four new laws were subsequently passed in New York by 1913. New labor laws made New York one of the most progressive states when it came to labor reform. A bill reducing the length of the standard work week was enacted. New laws required better building exits, fireproofing, sprinklers, fire extinguishers, fire alarms, better sanitation in the workplace, and a limit to the number of hours women and children could work.

The Triangle Shirtwaist Factory fire was the worst workplace disaster in New York City until the terrorist attacks of September 11, 2001. Today, the Asch Building is known as the Brown Building and is part of New York

University. It has been designated a National Historic Landmark.

12

Sampoong Department Store Collapse

1995

South Korea

"I wake up every morning and go out to look at the latest list of corpses found, and then I make the rounds in the hospital looking for my sister's corpse. I eat because I need my energy to go on, but it's like eating sand." — unidentified survivor

The Sampoong Department store was built between 1987 and 1989 in Seoul, South Korea. The land it was built upon was formerly a landfill on unstable ground. It was originally designed to be a four-story residential apartment building, but Lee Joon, of the Sampoong Group, changed the plans during construction to make the building a department store instead. Opening on July 7, 1990, the store attracted about 40,000 people a day over the next five years. It was one of the most fashionable shopping destinations in Seoul, and a favorite among the wives of the business and political elite.

In order to install escalators in the building for shoppers, a number of support columns needed to be removed. When the contractors refused to do this, Lee fired them and had his own building company finish the job.

The decision was made to add a fifth floor. Because zoning regulations did not permit the entire building to be a department store, this floor was to be a skating rink. Lee changed the plans to include eight restaurants instead. The construction company in charge of this phase of construction warned him that the structure was not designed to support a fifth floor. Lee fired this company, and another company was hired, which proceeded with the expansion. The concrete slab floor for the restaurants was heated by hot water pipes (because in traditional Korean restaurants, the customers sit on the floor), adding to the stress on the structure. The "eating gallery" was so popular among patrons that an artificial pond with a full-size windmill was soon added.

In April of 1995, cracks began to appear in the ceiling of the fifth floor. Some of the facilities and merchandise were moved from the fifth floor to the basement in response. On June 29, the number of cracks increased, and managers closed the top floor and shut off the air conditioners. Not wanting to lose the day's revenues, no warnings were given or evacuations ordered for the many shoppers in the building. The Sampoong Group executives, however, left the building as a precaution.

Engineers were brought in to evaluate the structure; they warned that the building was at risk for collapse. Shortly after noon, several loud bangs emanated from the top of the structure; the air conditioners had turned on, and the vibrations caused cracks in the slabs and columns to widen further. The cracks were examined, and some measured nearly four inches (10 cm) across. Nothing was done to warn occupants or evacuate the building.

At about 5:00 p.m. on June 29, 1995, the fifth floor began to sink, and employees blocked access to the fifth floor. The store was packed with customers, mostly upper-middle class housewives, but managers refused to close the store or evacuate shoppers to safety, although they did shut down the fourth floor. At 5:52, large cracking sounds could be heard, and employees began to sound alarms and evacuate customers. Before most people inside could escape, the roof gave way and the air conditioning units crashed down onto the fifth floor, which could not bear the load. The main columns supporting the structure collapsed and the entire south wing pancaked into the basement. More than 1,500 people were trapped; 937 were injured, and 502 were killed.

The formal investigation later revealed more factors which contributed to the collapse. The foundation was poorly-constructed and built in the unstable ground of a landfill. Testing revealed that substandard cement and poorly reinforced concrete had been used in the structure's ceilings and walls. The supporting columns, which had been reduced in number to accommodate the escalators, were only 24 inches (60 cm) wide, only three-quarters the diameter required. Also, the number of steel reinforcing bars embedded in the concrete was only eight, half the number required.

It was also found that, in order to install fire shields around the escalators to prevent the spread of fire, the supporting columns had been cut into, reducing their support strength. Along with the extra weight of the fifth-floor addition, the heavy restaurant equipment also contributed to the collapse.

The air conditioning units installed on the roof provided four times the load the roof was designed to support. To make matters worse, in 1993, the air conditioners had been moved because of noise complaints from neighbors. Instead of using a crane, they were dragged across the roof, further damaging the structure. Workmen noticed cracks in the roof while the units were being moved, and the cracks spread and widened over the course of the following two years.

Rescue crews arrived at the disaster site within minutes of the collapse. More than 200 survivors were pulled from the debris on the first day. Authorities were concerned that the rest of the building would come down on rescuers, so they were pulled back. Heavy equipment arrived the following day to remove debris and search for victims after the structure was stabilized with cables. The relatives of those missing protested the delays. On the third day, officials declared it was unlikely anyone was still alive, but three survivors were pulled from the wreckage 11, 13, and 17 days after the collapse. The final recovered survivor said that many had survived by drinking rainwater in the days that followed the disaster, but the other survivors had drowned in the water the fire department had been pouring on the collapsed structure to reduce the amount of dust in the air.

Lee Joon was charged with criminal negligence. His prison sentence of ten-and-a-half years was reduced to seven years when he appealed the ruling. He died days after his release in 2003. His son, Lee Han-Sang, the store's president, went to prison for seven years. Two city officials were convicted of taking bribes to overlook the shoddy construction and sentenced to three years imprisonment. Other officials were also sentenced for corruption, and some of the Sampoong executives, as well as officials at the construction company that built the structure, were also jailed. In total, 23 were jailed or fined. Settlements of about $350 million were ordered. The Lee family was stripped of all possessions to pay the claims and the Sampoong Group was disbanded. The Seoul city government offered compensation of more than $250,000 to the families of each of the victims.

The Sampoong Department Store disaster was the deadliest structure failure since a collapse of the seating section at the Circus Maximus in Rome, which killed approximately 13,000 people in about 140 A.D. It held this distinction for only six years until the collapse of New York's World Trade Center in 2001.

The disaster brought attention to rampant corruption in local governments in South Korea. Public demonstrations on the streets of Seoul, in response to the public's outrage over the bribery scandal and rampant shoddy building construction, went on for months. The staggering cost of South Korea's breakneck economic growth was examined and received much criticism. The nation's building regulations were reviewed and subsequently strengthened.

13

Collinwood School Fire

1908

Ohio, USA

"Oh, God, what have we done to deserve this?" —
witness

*"After the flames had died away, huge heaps of little
bodies, burned by the fire, and trampled into things of
horror told the tale as well as anybody need know it."* —
Chicago Tribune article, March 5, 1908

Often it takes many costly and deadly disasters before
changes are made to prevent further loss of life. Structure
fires have been a thorn in man's side for millennia, but it was
only in the last hundred years or so that significant
improvements in building codes, structural design, and
safety procedures have been implemented on a large scale.

Lake View School, a four-story masonry and wood
structure in the Cleveland, Ohio, neighborhood of
Collinwood, caught fire on Ash Wednesday, March 8, 1908.
An overheated steam pipe ignited a wooden support joist in
the basement, just under the main entrance. Oiled wooden
floors fueled the fire. The main stairwell acted as a chimney,
and the fire quickly consumed the school, giving the 366
children who attended the school just minutes to react.

Custodian Fritz Herter, who had four of his own
children in the school, quickly rang the fire gong, and
attempted to evacuate the building.

The school had no fire doors to contain flames. The few escape routes led to doors which were either locked or opened inward. One fire escape at the rear of the building operated properly, allowing some children to escape the conflagration. Some students died jumping from the upper story windows or were burned to death; others died from smoke inhalation. Most of the 175 who died, however, met their end in the main stairwell in a crush of panicking children trying to escape.

Collinwood's Police Chief, Charles G. McIlrath, who also had three children inside, was one of the first to arrive at the school. He later recalled terror-stricken faces peering out the windows, looking for help. Parents and first responders attempted to pull survivors from the 6-foot high mass of screaming children wedged inside the doors.

By the time a horse-drawn fire wagon arrived, the building was consumed in flames. The firefighters wouldn't have made much of a difference, though, as they didn't bring ladders to reach the second story windows, and there wasn't enough water pressure to fight the blaze. It was all over in 20 minutes. No survivors were pulled from the school once the floors collapsed and the fire had burned through the school.

Three of Herter's four children died in the blaze. McIlrath's oldest son, two teachers, and a rescuer were also lost; all four died trying to help youngsters get out of the building. Only about 80 students made it out of the building unhurt.

The disaster, a few years after the Iroquois Theatre fire, was one of several which led the U.S. to make improvements in fire safety: better fire exits, fire-resistant building materials, doors that swing out to aid in evacuations, and panic bars that open locked doors in an emergency. Better school inspections and strict fire prevention laws were soon adopted across the country.

What was left of Lake View School was torn down, and Collinwood Memorial Elementary School was built in its place. This new school was framed in steel, and other fire-resistant materials were used. Improved stairwells and emergency exits and a central alarm system were incorporated. Although this school has since been razed and a new one built in 2005 to replace it, students still participate in fire safety drills. They are taught about the lessons learned: that most of Lake View's students died because they panicked and blocked the exits.

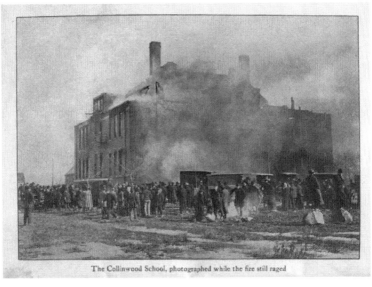

The Collinwood School, photographed while the fire still raged

Photo credit: Marshall Everett, Complete Story of the Collinwood School Disaster And How Such Horrors Can Be Prevented. N.G. Hamilton Publishing Co, 1908.

14

Aleksandr Suvorov Cruise Ship Disaster

1983

USSR/Russia

Details of some disasters are hard to come by because the government of the country in which they happen do not permit details to be reported, out of fear of ridicule, or national pride. We do know there was a disaster aboard a cruise ship, the *Aleksandr Suvorov*, in the Soviet Union in 1983, but reliable information is hard to come by even decades later.

The *Aleksandr Suvorov* is a four-deck river cruise ship, built in Czechoslovakia in 1981. She cruised up and down the Volga and Don rivers. A flagship of the Volga-Don Lines, she was based at Rostov-on-Don and had a capacity of 400 passengers.

On June 5, 1983, the *Aleksandr Suvorov* was sailing from Rostov to Moscow with 330 passengers and 65 crew and service staff. That evening, at about 10:00 p.m., in the cinema hall on the top deck, an auction was taking place; translation services were offered, which brought many of the passengers to the top deck. Sailing at full speed, 16 mph (25 kph, 13 knots), the ship was under the control of chief mate Vladimir Mitenkov and helmsman Uvarov in the deck house; Captain Vladimir Kleymenov was in his cabin for the evening. As it approached the railway bridge at Ulyanovsk, bridge controllers noticed the ship was heading for the sixth span of the bridge; only the second span was higher than the ship. They tried to reach the ship by radio, but there was no response. They then launched a warning flare, but it was too late to change course. The *Aleksandr Suvorov* struck the bridge, which sliced into the deck house and cinema hall, leaving only the lowest deck undamaged. The cinema hall, where most of the passengers were, was completely sheared off by a bridge girder.

Unfortunately, when the ship slammed into the bridge, a freight train was crossing the river. Four cars derailed from the impact and fell, dumping their contents of grain and coal onto the ship. The *Aleksandr Suvorov* continued another 1,000 feet (300 m) before coming to a stop. It took 40 minutes for rescue boats to reach the ship.

Shortly thereafter, the city was declared a closed city; no one was allowed to enter or leave Ulyanovsk. Residents were recruited for blood donations and to build makeshift coffins. The death toll stood at 177. Many of the survivors had serious avulsion wounds from the flying coal and grain; their skin was torn away and the underlying structure of tissue, muscles, tendons, and bones were exposed.

Investigators tested the remains of Mitenkov and Uvarov, who were killed instantly, but found they were sober at the time. Captain Kleymenov, who was retrieved from the water after the collision in a distraught state, was condemned to 10 years in prison for failing to prevent the collision; he was released after six.

Complaints had previously been made that the bridge was not lit properly by the railroad, making it nearly impossible to see in the dark. A switch tower on the bridge at the point of impact was similar to the navigation sign which marked the correct span under which ships could safely navigate, and, in the dark, the pilot apparently could not tell the difference.

The ship was restored and continues in service today.

15

Bhola Cyclone

1970

East Pakistan (Bangladesh)

"I cannot find words adequate to describe the holocaust which the cyclone and tidal bore have left in their trail. Nor can I adequately convey in words the suffering and the misery of those who have survived. Whole areas have been totally depopulated. In many areas of Patuakhali, Bhola, and Noakhali, barely 20 to 25 percent of the total population has survived. The survivors have lost their homes, their crops, their cattle; in fact they have lost all their worldly belongings. They are without clothes, without shelter and in many of the areas without any food or drinking water." —Sheikh Mujibur Rahman

Few disasters have caused the social and political upheaval that the Bhola cyclone, which struck East Pakistan (now Bangladesh), did in 1970 and 1971. The cyclone, one of the deadliest natural disasters in modern times, spawned a civil war, an international conflict, and resulted in the birth of a new nation.

A little political background is needed to understand what happened.

India spent more than two centuries under British rule. The Indian Independence Act of 1947 created two separate, independent dominions of the crown: India and Pakistan. In 1950, India became fully independent; Pakistan did so in 1956.

Bengal, the region at the head of the Bay of Bengal, was politically partitioned in 1947. The western part of the region, primarily Hindu, became the state of Bengal, India. The eastern section, primarily Muslim, then called East Bengal, joined with the Muslim dominion of Pakistan in 1956 to become the Islamic Republic of Pakistan. This independent nation consisted of two widely-separated areas, commonly called West Pakistan and East Pakistan.

East Pakistan bordered India on three sides, with the Bay of Bengal along its southern edge. It was one of the largest Pakistani states, the most populous state, and had the most powerful economy. However, it was separated from the rest of the country by about a thousand miles (1,600 km).

The coast at the northern end of the Bay of Bengal is quite vulnerable to tropical cyclones (the Indian Ocean equivalent of hurricanes and typhoons). The funneling coastal geography at the head of the bay, the low, flat terrain, when combined with a high astronomical tide, causes extreme storm surges when cyclones approach. Thirteen of the nineteen deadliest tropical cyclone disasters in the world through 1970 were in the Bay of Bengal, in India or what was East Pakistan. Ten cyclones since 1876 have had death tolls surpassing 5,000, with four killing more than 100,000.

After two cyclones had killed some 16,000 people in East Pakistan in 1960, the Pakistani government asked the U.S. for assistance in making plans to avert disaster again. The Pakistanis made some progress, but failed to carry out many of the recommendations the National Hurricane Center's director, Gordon Dunn, had made in the formal report.

East Pakistan was located in the Ganges River delta. Most of the country was near sea level. The Ganges delta is also prone to serious flooding. In an average year, 20% of the country is inundated by the annual river floods. It also happens to be one of the most densely populated regions on earth.

On November 5, 1970, Tropical Storm Nora crossed the Malay Peninsula and contributed to the development of a new cyclone in the Bay of Bengal. The storm remained almost stationary in open seas, but strengthened into a strong cyclone on November 11 and started moving north. It reached the equivalent of a Category 3 hurricane later that day, and made landfall in East Pakistan on November 12, 1970. Average winds were in excess of 140 mph (225 kph).

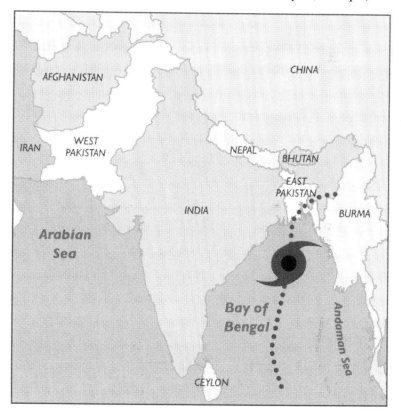

Landfall occurred about the same time as high tide. The storm surge and the high tide combined to raise water levels about 33 feet (10 m) above mean sea level. Many of the low-lying islands of the delta were inundated. The result was the deadliest tropical cyclone ever; somewhere between 300,000 and 500,000 people lost their lives. The island of Bhola took the brunt of the storm, with about 100,000 dead.

The Indian government had received numerous reports from ships in the Bay of Bengal, warning that a severe cyclone was moving toward the coast. Because relations between the Indians and the Pakistanis were strained, the information was not passed on to the Pakistanis. Many people in East Pakistan were taken by surprise when the storm hit. Only about 1% of the population sought refuge in reinforced buildings and storm shelters. More than half of the deaths were children under the age of 10, who were unable to save themselves. The storm was especially deadly because it struck during the night, when many people were sleeping and unable to reach safety.

According to Pakistani radio, there were no survivors on the 13 islands off the coast near Chittagong. In the city of Tazumuddin, 45% of the population of 167,000 was killed.

Where the storm made landfall, 85% of the homes were destroyed or severely damaged. The storm decimated the fishing industry; tens of thousands of fishermen were killed, and 9,000 fishing boats were destroyed. Agricultural losses were staggering, and 280,000 cattle drowned. The water supply was contaminated by the storm surge's sea water. Three months later, 75% of the population was still receiving food from relief workers, because the ability to harvest food locally had been destroyed. More than 3.6 million people were directly affected by the storm.

On November 16, the Pakistani President, General Yahya Khan, overflew the disaster zone and declared that no effort would be spared to provide relief to the people of East Pakistan. But, in the 10 days after the cyclone struck, the Pakistani government only provided one military aircraft and three crop-dusting aircraft to provide relief. A week after landfall, the president said the government had underestimated the magnitude of the disaster and had made "mistakes" in coordinating relief. The government later claimed they were refused permission by India to overfly that country to reach the stricken area. India denied this claim. By November 24, the president was in Dhaka coordinating relief missions.

On November 19, 50,000 people protested in the streets, and speakers demanded that the president resign. On November 22, 11 East Pakistani political leaders issued a statement charging the government with "gross neglect and utter indifference," and accused the president of playing down the disaster in the media. The opposition demanded his resignation, accusing him of bungling the relief operation.

National newspapers reported on the lack of relief coordination; at the same time, the government continued to issue reports stating that "relief operations are going smoothly." In January, thousands of survivors were still living out in the open, despite it being the coldest month of the year. The *Pakistan Observer* reported that in the hardest hit areas, they were unable to find any of the tents supplied by relief agencies to house victims. Survivors were given $55 USD ($325 in 2015 U.S. dollars) to rebuild, but were slow to issue building permits.

Despite the animosity between India and Pakistan, India was one of the first countries to offer relief aid. The Indian government offered military aircraft, helicopters, and boats, but Pakistan refused to allow India to send anything by air into East Pakistan, so supplies made their way slowly into the disaster zone by road. The coastal waters are so shallow that normal ships could not be used to distribute relief supplies. CARE halted aid shipments a week after the cyclone, unwilling to let the Pakistani government handle supply distribution. The Pakistani government also turned down an offer by the American Peace Corps to send volunteers.

The Awami League, a "pro-liberation" political party, was swept into power in December 1970 elections, winning 167 of 169 East Pakistani seats in the National Assembly (the party won no seats in West Pakistan), and 288 of 300 provincial assembly seats. The Awami League, led by Sheikh Mujibur Rahman, held enough seats to rule the national government. National political leaders in West Pakistan considered this unacceptable, as all of the national political power was in the hands of one province. The result was the Bangladesh Liberation War.

The Pakistani military junta, led by General Yahya Khan, began a military operation against Bengali nationalists on March 25, 1971. The junta overturned the election results, arrested Prime Minister-elect Sheikh Mujibur Rahman, banned East Pakistani political parties and newspapers, and declared martial law. East Pakistan formally seceded from Pakistan the following day.

The Pakistan Armed Forces conducted military raids and air strikes, committed widespread human rights abuses (massacres, murders, rape, and arson), and systematically eliminated liberation forces. It supported radical religious militias who contributed to the atrocities. During nine months of war, somewhere between 300,000 and 3,000,000 people were killed and as many as 400,000 women were victims of a systematic campaign of genocidal rape. The Bangladesh genocide is considered one of the five largest genocides of the twentieth century.

The widespread atrocities were particularly aimed at the minority Hindu population. Ten million refugees fled to India. A massive guerilla war was waged against national forces. The Pakistani government had underestimated the liberation movement, however, and in a few months rebel forces had seized control of much of the countryside. Soon the tide turned, and the provisional government and Awami League fled to India to lead the fight against the Pakistani Army through 1971. India, led by Prime Minister Indira Gandhi, provided diplomatic and military assistance.

The plight of Bangladeshi civilians led to worldwide outrage, but some of Pakistan's key allies, including U.S. President Richard Nixon, continued to support the West Pakistani junta.

On December 3, 1971, Pakistan launched a pre-emptive air strike on 11 northern India air bases, and India entered the war by siding with Bangladeshi nationalist forces. The Indo-Pakistani War of 1971 lasted just 13 days, and is one of the shortest wars in history. It ended with a decisive Indian victory.

In those 13 days, forces clashed on both eastern and western fronts. On December 16, the Eastern Command of the Pakistani Armed Forces were overwhelmed and surrendered, and the new nation of Bangladesh was born. It was the seventh most populous nation on earth.

India took nearly a third of Pakistan's military as prisoners. Pakistan lost more than half its population when Bangladesh was liberated, as well as a significant portion of its economy. India had clearly established dominance of the subcontinent.

Pakistanis, who had been fed propaganda by the military junta indicating that Pakistan was winning the war, were humiliated when Pakistan surrendered so quickly. Demonstrations and protests erupted throughout the country.

To deter another armed invasion from India, Pakistan embarked on a secret atomic bomb program. India beat Pakistan to the punch by conducting a surprise nuclear test in 1974. A second bomb was tested in 1998, and a few weeks later, from May 28–30, 1998, Pakistan detonated five nuclear devices.

The Bhola cyclone resulted in new plans by relief organizations to mount significant relief operations in the event of a massive disaster anywhere in the world. In 1972, a cyclone warning system was inaugurated in Bangladesh, and a public awareness campaign was launched to teach the nation's people how to survive tropical storms. Extensive training programs were launched to prepare emergency personnel.

Seven of the nine deadliest weather events in the world in the 20th century were tropical cyclones striking Bangladesh. In the 30 years after the Bhola cyclone, more than 200 cyclone shelters were built in Bangladesh. The next destructive cyclone, Cyclone Gorky in 1991, resulted in warnings to the population two to three days before landfall. Despite this cyclone being a Category 5 storm and quite a bit more destructive, considerably fewer deaths occurred, although the toll of 138,000 dead is still staggering.

16

Halifax Explosion

1917

Nova Scotia, Canada

"The house began to shake and it seemed to get dark and then there was a terrific crash. The doors and windows came flying in — glass everywhere. I remember seeing a boy standing in the frame of the doorway of a house.... He said he was the only one left." —Wilfrid Creighton, survivor

During the First World War, Halifax, Nova Scotia, Canada, was an important port for Trans-Atlantic crossings. The British Royal Navy used Halifax as its North American base of operations. In response to repeated German U-boat attacks, the convoy system had been adopted to protect ships and cargoes. Merchant and troop transport ships were protected by British cruisers and destroyers. All neutral ships bound for North American ports were required to report to Halifax for inspection.

The city is home to one of the deepest and largest natural harbors in the world. By 1917, a growing naval fleet was stationed in Halifax, and the city's industrial activity, military presence, and population was expanding. The population had surpassed 50,000, and Halifax was now the largest city in the Maritime Provinces.

A six-mile (9.6-km) long strait called The Narrows connected the Atlantic Ocean and the port with Bedford Basin, which was protected by antisubmarine nets. On either side of The Narrows were the cities of Dartmouth (on the east) and Halifax (on the west bank).

On December 3, 1917, a Norwegian ship, SS *Imo*, en route from the Netherlands to New York, where relief supplies would be loaded and then delivered to Belgium, arrived in Halifax for inspection. The *Imo* was cleared to continue on her voyage on December 5, but her load of coal was not delivered until late in the day. By the time the fuel was loaded, the antisubmarine nets had been raised for the night, so the ship had to wait until the next morning, December 6, to depart.

Meanwhile, a French cargo ship, SS *Mont-Blanc*, arrived late on December 5. The ship was fully loaded with TNT and picric acid (both are explosives), benzole (a high-octane fuel), and guncotton (now known as nitrocellulose, a highly flammable propellant and explosive). The *Mont-Blanc* intended to join a convoy gathering in Bedford Basin, bound for France to join the war effort. However, she arrived too late and the antisubmarine nets had been raised. Although dangerous cargoes were not allowed into the port before the war, the threat from German U-boats was too high and the *Mont-Blanc* was allowed into the harbor. The ship flew no flags warning of her hazardous cargo, since it would then be a prime target for an attack by a German submarine.

When traveling in and out of Bedford Basin through The Narrows, ships were expected to keep to the right side of the channel and keep their speed below five knots.

The submarine nets protecting the harbor were opened at about 7:30 a.m. on December 6. The *Imo* was granted clearance to leave Bedford Basin. She entered the Narrows well above the speed limit to make up for the delay in loading her fuel. She met an American tramp steamer, SS *Clara*, which was being piloted up the wrong side of the harbor, and the pilots agreed to pass starboard-to-starboard (on the left side of each other). After passing the *Clara*, the *Imo* was forced farther to port by a tugboat, *Stella Maris*, traveling up the center of the channel. The captain of the *Stella Maris* saw the *Imo* approaching at high speed and ordered the boat farther to port, along the western shore, to avoid a collision.

The *Mont-Blanc* also started moving up The Narrows toward Bedford Basin at 7:30. The captain, while watching for ferries traveling back-and-forth between Halifax and Dartmouth, saw the *Imo* approaching on the east side of the channel when it was still 0.75 miles (1.21 km) ahead. The captain gave a short blast of the whistle to indicate he had the right of way; the *Imo* responded with two short blasts, indicating it would not yield to the *Mont-Blanc*. The captain of the *Mont-Blanc* ordered the engines cut and angled the ship to starboard, hoping the Imo would move to its starboard, where it was supposed to be traveling. He signaled with another short blast of the whistle, but *Imo* again gave two short blasts and did not change her speed or direction.

The series of signals were drawing the attention of sailors on nearby ships, and they gathered to watch *Imo* bear down on *Mont-Blanc*. Both ships cut their engines, and *Mont-Blanc* was steered hard to port to pass to the left of *Imo*. When the two ships were almost parallel to each other, the *Imo* sent out three signal blasts, indicating it was reversing its engines. Because the ship was cargoless and sat high in the water, and therefore was difficult to steer, the maneuver caused the *Imo's* bow to swing into the side of the *Mont-Blanc*.

The ships collided at 8:45. The damage to the *Mont-Blanc* was relatively minor, but the impact knocked barrels on the deck filled with benzole over, which quickly spilled into the ship's hold. The *Imo* restarted her engines to pull away from the nine-foot (2.7-m) gash; the movement created sparks inside the *Mont-Blanc*'s hull, igniting the benzole vapors. The fire traveled up the water line to the benzole spewing from the damaged drums on the *Mont-Blanc*'s decks, and the fire was quickly out of control. The captain of the *Mont-Blanc* ordered the crew to abandon ship, fearing the ship would explode.

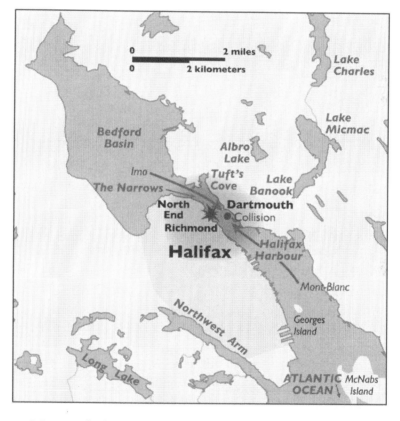

Many of the citizens of Halifax moved toward the harbor, mesmerized by the raging fire. Others watched from their doors and windows.

As the *Mont-Blanc*'s crew made their way to shore in

lifeboats, they tried to warn others on the water to stay away from the ship, but they could not be heard in the chaos. The abandoned *Mont-Blanc* drifted to the west side of the channel and beached herself at Pier 6. The fire spread to the pier's wooden pilings.

The tug *Stella Maris* immediately anchored her barges and responded to the fire, but the crew quickly realized they did not have enough equipment to fight the blaze and backed away. They were then assisted by the crews of two other ships, HMS *Highflyer* and HMCS *Niobe*, who attempted to secure a line to the *Mont-Blanc* and pull it away from the pier. Before they could accomplish this, the fire ignited the *Mont-Blanc*'s highly explosive cargo.

The blast occurred at 9:04. The *Mont-Blanc* was completely blown to pieces; shards of her hull sailed 1,000 feet (300 m) into the air. A blast wave traveled outward at more than 3,300 feet (1,000 m) per second. The shock wave traveled through the earth at 23 times the speed of sound and could be felt at Cape Breton (129 miles, 207 km away) and Prince Edward Island (110 miles, 180 km away). White-hot pieces of metal rained down on Halifax and Dartmouth. An area of 400 acres (160 hectares) was completely obliterated. The concussive shock snapped trees, flattened buildings, bent iron rails, and grounded other vessels in the area. A white cloud billowed 20,000 feet (6,100 m) into the air over the city.

The explosion vaporized such a large amount of water in the harbor that the harbor floor was momentarily exposed. As water rushed to fill the void, a 60-foot (18-m) tsunami formed. The tsunami carried the *Imo* onto the shore at Dartmouth (where it stayed until spring), and totally obliterated a community of Mi'kmaq First Nations people living at Tuft's Cove.

The forward 90 mm gun from the *Mont-Blanc* melted in the explosion and landed 3.5 miles (5.6 km) north of the center of the explosion; a half-ton piece of her anchor landed 2 miles (3.2 km) to the south. Large factories made of brick and stone near Pier 6 were reduced to rubble, and most of the workers were killed. Every building within 1.6 miles (2.6 km), numbering 12,000, was destroyed or badly damaged.

SS Imo *aground on the Dartmouth side of the harbor after the explosion.*

The blast killed almost everyone on the *Stella Maris*, *Highflyer*, and *Niobe*, but all but one of the *Mont-Blanc* crew survived because by the time the ship exploded, they had furiously rowed to shore and had escaped the waterfront, knowing what was about to happen. One of the crew was struck by a projectile and killed as he ran through the streets away from the burning ship.

More than 1,600 people were killed instantly; 9,000 were injured, 300 of whom later died from their injuries. Hundreds of people who had been watching from their homes were blinded when the blast shattered their windows. The blast knocked over stoves and lamps, igniting fires all over the city. In the North End neighborhood of Halifax, entire city blocks burned, trapping residents in their homes. Survivors reported victims, some headless, hanging out of windows or tangled in telegraph lines. More Nova Scotians died in the explosion than were killed in World War I.

The view across Halifax, with Dartmouth and SS Imo *in the background.*

It could have been worse. A dispatcher for the Intercolonial Railway, working in the rail yard about 750 feet (230 m) from Pier 6, learned of the *Mont-Blanc's* fire and its hazardous cargo and continued to send urgent telegraph messages to approaching trains. Incoming trains were stopped away from the harbor and hundreds of lives were saved. The dispatcher stayed at his post and was killed in the explosion.

Other stations along the Intercolonial Railway heard the dispatcher's warnings and immediately launched emergency responses from outside the city. Rescue trains were dispatched from all over eastern Canada and the United States, but a blizzard delayed their arrival in Halifax.

The Halifax Fire Department, attempting to extinguish the fire aboard the *Mont-Blanc*, lost nine members when the ship exploded. Soon, rescue personnel arrived on rescue trains from all over eastern Canada to assist the people of Halifax, where any able-bodied person with a vehicle was already at work collecting the injured and transporting them to hospitals, and collecting dead bodies. Fire departments responding from other cities soon found, however, that their hoses could not be connected to Halifax's water supply because the connections were different, so much of the equipment that arrived was useless.

The city's hospitals were quickly overwhelmed. A military hospital at Camp Hill admitted 1,400 injured survivors on the first day alone.

The Royal Canadian Navy and the British Royal Navy had more than two dozen ships in the harbor when the explosion occurred. Some of these ships dispatched teams ashore to medically assist survivors and take the wounded aboard. The U.S. Coast Guard also responded and dispatched landing parties. The USS *Tacoma*, an American cruiser passing by Halifax in the Atlantic Ocean, was so jolted by the blast wave that the ship went to general quarters. The *Tacoma* and the USS *Von Steuben* could see the rising column of smoke from the explosion, and steamed to the port to render aid. The American steamship *Old Colony*, which was docked in Halifax but suffered little damage, was quickly converted to a hospital ship, staffed by medical personnel from American and British navy vessels.

Survivors feared that the explosion was the result of a German air attack, and local military installations initially went on alert to protect the city. As soon as the origin of the blast was determined, the troops switched to rescue operations. However, the *Halifax Herald* continued to report the rumors for some time. German survivors were rounded up and put in prison immediately after the explosion. The Norwegian helmsman of the *Imo,* seriously injured in the blast, was arrested under suspicion of being a German spy, but was released when it was determined that the letter in his possession was in fact written in Norwegian, not German. When the real cause of the disaster was understood, the fear of German attack faded away.

Buildings across the city suffered serious structural damage, with most windows blown out.

Survivors soon feared a second blast was imminent. A fire broke out at the Wellington Barracks ammunition magazine. Although the fire was quickly extinguished, steam continued to shoot into the air. Police ordered an evacuation, and many people fled their homes. Rescue efforts were hampered by rumors of another imminent explosion for more than two hours.

One of the trains that was warned and stopped just outside the city before the blast was only slightly damaged, and entered the city to render aid. Passengers and soldiers aboard the train helped dig out survivors and loaded the injured onto the train. It left Halifax for Truro at 1:30 p.m. By nightfall, a dozen rescue trains had reached Halifax.

The Halifax Relief Commission was formed by leading citizens before noon. Its mission was to organize medical relief, supply transportation, provide food and shelter, and pay for medical treatment and burials. The commission continued operating until 1976, assisting in the reconstruction process as well as paying pensions to survivors.

A blizzard struck Halifax that evening and continued through the following day, covering the city in 16 inches (41 cm) of heavy snow. People trapped in collapsed buildings died from exposure. Rescue trains from the rest of Canada and the U.S. became stuck in snowdrifts. Telegraph lines, which had been hastily repaired after the blast, were knocked down again. Although relief efforts were delayed because of the storm, the snow helped to put out fires still burning around the city.

With 6,000 people now homeless and 25,000 living in damaged buildings, construction of temporary shelters began almost immediately. The industrial section of the city lay in ruins, and the dockyard was heavily damaged. By late January, the number of homeless had dropped to about 5,000 because of reconstruction activities. By March 1, 1918,

832 modern flats had been constructed for those without shelter, and 3,000 damaged homes had been repaired. The North End neighborhood, which bore the brunt of the explosion, had been a working class community before the disaster; its reconstruction created a new neighborhood of better-built homes, businesses, and parks. The North End has since become an upscale neighborhood and shopping district.

The Wreck Commissioner's Inquiry was launched to investigate the circumstances of the collision and explosion. Despite the fact that the *Imo* was operating on the wrong side of the channel, the inquiry blamed the crew of the *Mont-Blanc* for not avoiding the collision at all cost given the dangerous nature of the ship's cargo. The captain and pilot of the *Mont-Blanc*, as well as the Royal Canadian Navy's chief officer in charge of the harbor, were charged with manslaughter and criminal negligence. The charges against the captain and pilot were dropped by a Nova Scotia Supreme Court justice. The officer in charge of the harbor was acquitted by a jury in a trial that lasted less than a day.

A civil litigation trial determined that the *Mont-Blanc* was at fault, but appeals to the Supreme Court of Canada and the Judicial Committee of the Privy Council in London led to the conclusion that both ships were equally at fault. In the end, no one was ever convicted of any crime or prosecuted for any action that led to the disaster.

With about 5,900 people suffering from eye injuries and 41 losing their sight permanently, physicians learned how to better care for damaged eyes. Halifax became internationally known as a center for expert care for the blind. The specialty of pediatric care was given a boost by surgeons who noted the lack of coordinated care for the large number of children injured in the blast. Other medical advances were made in the study of emergency medicine, psychology, reconstructive surgery, and prosthetics because of the disaster.

The disaster led to the strengthening of international maritime standards, as well as new standards for detailed reporting of cargo, regulations on handling dangerous goods, and harbor traffic control. Cities throughout North America formed Emergency Measures Organizations (EMOs) to create disaster and emergency plans. New standards for equipment, such as fire hose connections, ensured that equipment would be usable in other municipalities.

The *Imo* was repaired and returned to service as the *Guvernøren*, a whale oil tanker, in 1920. On November 30, 1921, the captain fell down drunk, and, with nobody at the wheel, the ship grounded on rocks off the Falkland Islands. The ship was unsalvageable and was abandoned.

The Halifax explosion was the largest man-made blast to occur until the advent of nuclear weapons. It released energy equal to about 2.9 kilotons of TNT. (For reference, the Hiroshima nuclear blast in 1945 was equal to 12–15 kilotons of TNT.) For years, the Halifax explosion was the standard by which other large blasts were measured. In fact, when Hiroshima was bombed in 1945, *Time* reported that the nuclear blast was seven times that of the Halifax explosion. Scientists in the Manhattan Project, which created the first nuclear weapons, studied the Halifax explosion in order to understand the effects of huge blasts.

17

Big Bayou Canot Train Wreck

1993

Alabama, USA

"Forget the shoes. We need to get off now!" —R.C.
Sproul to his wife as fire spread toward their coach

On September 22, 1993, the towboat *Mauvilla* was
pushing a barge loaded with coal, steel slabs, iron pellets,
and cement up the Mobile River just northeast of Mobile,
Alabama. The pilot, Willie Odom, was lost in thick fog and
believed he was still in the main channel of the Mobile River.
Unfortunately, he had made a wrong turn and was moving
up an unnavigable channel, Big Bayou Canot.

Crossing the Big Bayou Canot was a CSX Transportation
rail bridge. The bridge has been designed to be converted
into a swing bridge, but that part of the design was never
implemented. Therefore, the end of the span had never been
adequately secured to prevent unintended lateral
movement.

At 2:45 a.m., the barge struck the span in the fog and
forced one end of the span about three feet (0.9 m) out of
alignment, severely kinking the track.

Eight minutes later, at 2:53 a.m., Amtrak's Sunset
Limited passenger train traveling from Los Angeles to
Miami reached the bridge, traveling at 78 mph (125 kph).
The train was pulled by three locomotives and carried 220
passengers and crew. When the train hit the displaced span,
part of the bridge collapsed into the water. The first

locomotive sailed 240 feet (73 m) through the air and embedded itself into the opposite riverbank; its fuel tank ruptured and exploded. The other two locomotives, the baggage car, and dormitory car plunged into the burning fuel spill. Two of the six passenger cars also derailed and plunged into the 30-foot (9-m) deep water. Forty-two passengers and five crew members were killed, most by drowning, and some by fire and smoke inhalation; 103 were injured.

Survivors had to wait three hours for help to arrive. The accident scene was in such a remote area in the Mobile River delta that it was accessible only by water or rail. A freight train following the passenger train was warned by radio of the derailment and had to back up for an hour to Mobile to clear the tracks so a rescue train could be sent.

The rescue train had three coaches filled with first responders. Survivors of the crash were loaded onto the train, which then returned to Mobile after an hour-long ride in reverse.

The Sunset Limited train had been delayed in New Orleans to repair an air conditioning unit, putting the train 30 minutes behind schedule. If the train had been operating on schedule, it would have passed over the bridge before it was struck by the barge.

Although the bridge had been displaced three feet, the rails did not break. If they had broken, the track circuit would have been broken and signals would have alerted the engineer that there were issues with the track ahead. Instead, the engineer had green signals, indicating that all was well.

It was later determined that the towboat pilot had not been trained how to properly read radar. Odom believed he was still on the main river channel and had identified the bridge's radar signal return as another tugboat. He planned to use it as temporary mooring until the fog cleared. The *Mauvilla* did not have a working compass or navigation charts of the river aboard; the charts had been left behind at the pilot's house. The National Transportation Safety Board also blamed the U.S. Coast Guard for the lack of sufficient standards for tugboat operator licensing. Willie Odom had only received his pilot's license a few months earlier after failing the exam seven times.

Nonetheless, Odom was later found to be not criminally liable for the accident. It was determined that no state laws had been violated. Odom gave up his piloting license to avoid a hearing.

The Big Bayou Canot disaster is the deadliest accident in Amtrak's history and the deadliest rail disaster in the U.S. since an accident in New Jersey in 1958.

18

The Beer and Pretzel Stampede at Khodynka Field

1896

Russia

"Saturday. Until now, everything was going, thank God, like clockwork, but today there was a great mishap. The crowd staying overnight at Khodynka, awaiting the start of the distribution of lunch and mugs pushed against buildings and there was a terrible crush, and awful to say trampled around 1300 people!! I found out about it at 10 1/2 hours before the report by [minister of war] Vannovski; a disgusting impression was left by this news. At 12 1/2 we had lunch and then Alix [Czarina] and I went to Khodynka to be present at this sad national holiday." —from the diary of Tsar Nicholas II

To celebrate the coronation of Russian Emperor Nicholas II four days earlier, a large banquet was planned for the people of Moscow on May 30, 1896. The government built a large complex of pubs, buffet stations, and theaters in Khodynka Field to serve the guests. Before the coronation, Khodynka Field had been the site of military barracks; it was also the site of celebrations for the coronation of Alexander III in 1883. Because it was a training ground for troop movements, the terrain was crossed by trenches and was pitted with holes. Makeshift bridges and barricades were built to accommodate the expected crowds.

The evening before, crowds began to form upon hearing the rumor that they would receive coronation gifts from the

Tsar: a bread roll, a piece of sausage, pretzels, gingerbread, and a commemorative enamel cup with beer.

By morning, thousands had gathered outside the gates; estimates of the crowd are as high as a half million people. Rumors spread through the crowd that there was not enough beer and pretzels to go around. Another rumor spread that the cups contained a gold coin. The crowd pushed forward, through the barricades holding them off the field, resulting in a crush of people and then a stampede as people tried to flee. Most of the victims were trampled or suffocated in the trenches, from which they couldn't escape. The death toll reached 1,389, and another 1,300 were injured.

The festivities continued as planned, however. Because of the size of the crowd, most attending the coronation celebration were unaware that anything tragic had happened. Tsar Nicholas and his wife Alexandra were told about the stampede hours later. At 2:00 p.m., he appeared on the balcony of the Tsar's Pavilion in the middle of Khodynka Field and addressed the crowds; all evidence of the disaster had been removed from the field by that time.

Nicholas chose to skip the festive ball scheduled for that evening out of respect for the victims, but his advisors convinced him to attend for diplomatic reasons. The following day, Nicholas and Alexandra visited the injured as they lay in hospital beds. The Empress was so distressed from the tragedy that she later suffered a miscarriage; the baby boy would have been next in line for the throne.

Over the next several days, bodies were moved by wagons to the morgues, where they were stacked like firewood and covered with canvas and sacks.

In response to the disaster, the Russian government provided aid to the families of the dead and some minor officials were dismissed from their posts. The official response was considered paltry. The government was blamed for negligence, adding to the public mood that ignited the Russian Revolution of 1905, which brought about constitutional reform to address problems within the country.

In the early 1900s, Khodynka Field was converted to an airfield, and the first powered Russian flight took place there in 1910. The field is now home to the main headquarters of Aeroflot (the national airline of Russia), the National Aviation and Space Museum, an ice arena, and a large shopping mall.

Nicholas II would be the last Russian Emperor; he abdicated his crown during the Russian Revolutions of 1917.

19

European Heatwave

2003

Europe

"Heat waves are slow, silent, and invisible killers of silent and invisible people." —Eric Klinenberg, sociologist

Persistent heatwaves, while not typically considered major hazards, can trigger high death tolls in areas that are not prepared for such extreme temperatures. The 2003 European heatwave is a recent example of this phenomenon. The death toll from the heatwave, which lasted from June to August, was about 70,000—an extreme number of deaths from a natural disaster in the developed world during modern times.

It was the hottest summer in Europe since 1540. In some areas, the extreme heat broke records that had stood for centuries. Temperatures hit 100°F (37.8°C) in the Netherlands; 113.2°F (45.1°C) in Spain; 101.3°F (38.5°C) in the U.K.; 106.7°F (41.5°C) in Switzerland; 104.7°F (40.4°C) in Germany; 114.8°F (46.0°C) in Italy; 118°F (48°C) in Portugal; and more than 104°F (40°C) in France. The heatwave led to severe health crises across the continent.

Worst hit was France, which typically has mild summers and cool nights. Many homes are built of stone, concrete, or brick, and therefore do not normally heat up quickly, so they are not equipped with air conditioning. During this heatwave, temperatures remained stiflingly hot during the night, so there was no chance for structures and the people inhabiting them to cool down.

The administration of French President Jacques Chirac and Prime Minister Jean-Pierre Raffarin blamed French tradition for the death toll, which reached 14,802. Most of the dead were elderly and/or disabled. Many companies traditionally close in August and many families go on vacation. Because so many families are gone for the month, physicians also use this time to go on their vacations. The French 35-hour work week also limited the time that physicians who remained behind were allowed to work. The result was that many elderly people were left behind in their stifling homes, without the support of relatives and the full health care system.

Because heatwaves of this magnitude are so rare in Europe, residents did not know how to react to the heat. Those living alone were far more likely to succumb to the heat than those in nursing homes. Bodies were stored in refrigerated warehouses because the morgues were not able to handle the sheer number of casualties. Many bodies were not claimed for weeks, when their relatives finally returned from vacation. By September, 57 bodies still hadn't been claimed in metropolitan Paris and were buried.

The government had drawn up detailed plans for dealing with a variety of natural and man-made disasters, but high temperatures hadn't been considered a major hazard worthy of such planning. There was no government plan in place to deal with the crisis. French health authorities weren't fully aware of the crisis as it unfolded, and the government was slow to respond. There was no public recall of doctors on vacation. The death toll led to internal criticism of French traditions and society, especially the tendency to leave the elderly behind at home during vacation season without anyone looking after them.

The cities of the American Midwest had learned eight years earlier that heatwaves could be very deadly. The July 1995 heatwave killed about 750 people in Chicago over five days. Others died in St. Louis, Missouri, and Milwaukee, Wisconsin. By the time anyone realized there were mass casualties from the heat, the heatwave had ended. Larger cities in the Midwest subsequently drew up contingency plans for dealing with extreme temperatures, including public cooling stations, public awareness campaigns, and "check on your neighbor" pleas via media announcements. The change in policies greatly reduced the number of deaths in the 2012 Midwest heatwave, which was considerably more severe, but only resulted in the deaths of 82 people.

French vacationers head to the beach in 2003, attempting to escape the extreme heat.

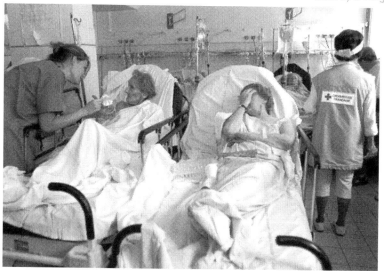

Elderly French citizens are treated for heat-related illnesses during the 2003 heatwave.

20

The Great Smog of '52

1952

United Kingdom

"We eventually got to Kingston at five in the morning, absolutely black as sweeps. As it was so cold — for fog brings the cold with it — I was wearing a woolly yellow scarf and that too was pitch black with soot and muck. Our faces were black, our noses were black and everything was filthy — and we were exhausted, of course." —Barbara Fewster, who walked home 16 miles in heels, guiding her fiancé in his car

On December 4, 1952, a temperature inversion formed over London, trapping cold, stagnant air near the ground under a layer of warmer air. This weather phenomenon forms a layer of fog near the surface. In this instance, the fog mixed with airborne pollutants to form a thick layer of smog (fog laden with soot) that persisted for five days.

Unusually cold weather preceded the smog event, so Londoners were burning more coal to keep warm than they usually did. In the post-war years, the U.K. was exporting the better-quality hard coal, which burns cleaner, and using low-grade coal which emitted larger quantities of sulfur dioxide when burned. Many of the power plants around the city were also coal-burning plants.

The coal soot in the air was worsened by pollution from vehicle exhaust, especially from diesel buses, which were by then being widely used after the electric tram system had been abandoned by the summer of 1952. To make matters worse, prevailing winds had brought more polluted air across the English Channel from heavily industrialized Continental Europe.

The fog, chimney smoke, vehicle exhaust, and industrial pollutants formed a thick smog that covered the city for days. The absence of wind over the five-day stretch increased the concentration of particulate matter in the air while preventing its dispersal. The increased emissions of sulfur dioxide gave the smog a yellow-black hue, giving the smog event the nickname "pea souper."

Despite Londoners being accustomed to dense fog, this event was far denser and lasted longer than any previous smog event. Driving or walking became nearly impossible as visibility was reduced to a few yards. Public transportation, as well as the ambulance service, shut down for the duration of the event. The lack of traffic contributed to the thick smog because the usual traffic patterns, which would have the effect of thinning the concentration of particles by moving the air, had ceased. Pedestrians were unable to see sidewalks and curbs. In some areas of the city, people could not see their own feet. At night, the incandescent bulbs still in use in 1952 were unable to penetrate the fog, making walking anywhere impossible.

The thick smog also penetrated indoors. Visibility in large, enclosed spaces was reduced to the point that theaters, movie houses, and sports venues had to cancel events. The smog even contributed to a rise in the crime rate, as thieves used the reduced visibility to get away with break-ins as well as robberies of those trying to make their way in the darkness.

Finally, on December 10, winds blew the pollution out into the North Sea.

Much like the rest of Europe in the heatwave of 2003, authorities were not aware until later how deadly the event had been. Within a few weeks, medical statistics showed the upwards of 4,000 people had died because of the smog, and 100,000 were sickened. Most of the victims were children, the elderly, or already had respiratory problems. Most deaths were due to respiratory and cardiac distress. More recent research indicates that the death toll was closer to 12,000. It was the worst pollution event in the history of the U.K.

The view in central London at 2:00 p.m. during the Great Smog of '52.

The event helped trigger the modern environmental movement, as man-made smog was now recognized for what it was: a lethal killer. New regulations were announced, including the Clean Air Act of 1956, restricting the use of dirty fuels. Homeowners received financial incentives to replace their coal-burning furnaces and stoves with cleaner alternatives.

21

Cocoanut Grove Fire

1942

Massachusetts, USA

"The entire doorway was a sheet of flames. I think I was the last person to come out that door alive." —Howard A. Jones, Jr.

The Cocoanut Grove nightclub in Boston, Massachusetts, was located in a complex of bars, lounges, and dining establishments in a building converted from a garage and warehouse. Decorated in a South Seas tropical paradise motif, the club boasted artificial palm trees made of flammable paper, heavy draperies, satin canopies hanging from the ceiling, and heavy use of rattan and bamboo. Flammable decorations covered many of the exit signs.

Owner Barnet "Barney" Welansky, who claimed to be connected to the Boston mafia and to Boston Mayor Maurice J. Tobin, had concealed exits with decorations and furnishings, locked exits, and even bricked over one of the emergency exits to keep customers from leaving without paying.

On November 28, 1942, it was estimated that over a thousand people were inside the club, which had a maximum legal capacity of 460. In the basement's Melody Lounge, newly opened for just eight days, a 16-year-old busboy, Stanley Tomaszewski, was replacing a lightbulb (reportedly removed by a young man so he could kiss his date in a more private setting). Stanley dropped the bulb, and because he couldn't see well in the dimly-lit lounge, lit a match in order to retrieve the bulb. Witnesses reported the artificial palm tree canopy over the tables quickly ignited.

The flames quickly spread along the decorations covering the ceilings and walls, engulfing hallways and other lounges. The lights went out and a yellowish-blue fireball swept up the stairs and through the main dance floor while the orchestra played. Within five minutes, the entire club was burning.

Patrons tried to flee through the main entrance, which was a single revolving door; the panicked crowd jammed the door completely, and the bodies piled up. Other doors that were unlocked opened inwards, and bodies piled up at those exits, too.

All told, 492 people were killed in the fire, the deadliest nightclub fire in history. It was the second-deadliest building fire in U.S. history; only the Iroquois Theatre fire killed more. One hundred sixty-six more were injured in the Cocoanut Grove.

Firefighters, during the building cleanup after the blaze, found dead patrons sitting in their seats with drinks in their hands; the fire and toxic smoke spread so fast, there wasn't time to react. Many victims were found with white foam on their lips; this baffled the doctors in 1942, but has since been recognized as the byproduct of breathing the highly toxic smoke.

Owner Barney Welansky was convicted of 19 counts of manslaughter and sentenced to 12–15 years in prison. He was pardoned by Gov. Tobin (the former Boston mayor) less than four years later. The busboy, Stanley Tomaszewski, was exonerated because the fire code violations and the highly combustible furnishings were not his fault. The official investigation listed the ignition source as "unknown." In the 1990s, researcher Charles Kenney, a former Boston firefighter, concluded that methyl chloride, a highly flammable gas propellant used in refrigeration systems, contributed to the flashover (Freon, more commonly used, was in short supply due to the war effort).

Fire laws were again tightened within a year after the blaze, and codes were rewritten to include larger bars and restaurants, not just theaters. Revolving doors were required to be collapsible or flanked by outward opening doors with panic bars. Exit doors were required to swing outwards; exit signs were required to be visible even in heavy smoke and to have an independent power supply. Some states established commissions with the power to levy fines or close down businesses who did not meet the new stricter regulations. Before long, these regulations evolved into federal fire laws and code restrictions for public buildings, clubs and restaurants, and theaters.

Surviving victims at local hospitals were treated with pioneering techniques for treating burns, and a recently established local blood bank was widely used. A new antibiotic, penicillin, was used to treat burn victims; in fact, Cocoanut Grove survivors were some of the first people to receive penicillin. Some of the earliest research on post-traumatic stress disorder was conducted on those who had survived the fire.

Highly flammable materials in nightclubs continue to be the cause of many deadly fires, even in the 21st century. One hundred people died at The Station, a nightclub in West Warwick, Rhode Island, in 2003 when pyrotechnics ignited acoustic foam on stage. In Perm, Russia, more than 150 died in 2009 when fireworks ignited the ceiling and its willow twig covering at the Lame Horse nightclub. The Wuwang Club fire in Shenzhen, China, killed 43 when fireworks ignited the ceiling in 2008. Another 242 people were killed and 630 injured in Santa Maria, Brazil, at the Kiss nightclub in 2013 when band members lit fireworks. The República Cromañón nightclub fire killed 194 in Buenos Aires, Argentina, in 2004; a pyrotechnic flare ignited foam in the ceiling. There were another 67 fatalities at the Santika Club in Bangkok, Thailand, on New Year's Day in 2009; it is thought that a midnight fireworks display ignited the roof. On October 30, 2015, at least 27 people died and 180 were injured in Bucharest, Romania, at the Colectiv nightclub; stage pyrotechnics ignited the polystyrene décor, and the crowd panicked and stampeded to get out of the club's only exit.

22

Disasters at the Hajj

Saudi Arabia

*"I saw people jumping over each other. The bodies were
piled up. I couldn't count them, they were too many."* —
Suad Abu Hamada, Egyptian pilgrim and witness to the
2006 stampede

All Muslims are required to take part in the Hajj, an
annual pilgrimage to the holy city of Mecca, Saudi Arabia, at
least once in their life if they are physically and financially
able to make the journey. Participating in the Hajj is one of
the five pillars, or duties, of Islam. The Hajj demonstrates
Muslims' submission to God (Allah), and is a symbol of the
solidarity of the faithful. It is considered the largest annual
gathering of people in the world, as two to three million
followers descend on the city each year for the week-long
event.

During the Hajj, a tradition with roots that trace back
four thousand years to the time of Abraham, hundreds of
thousands join processions and perform a series of rituals.
Each person walks seven times counter-clockwise around
the Ka'aba, the black cube-shaped structure that is the most
sacred site in Islam, toward which all Muslims pray. They
must travel seven times back and forth between Al-Safa and
Al-Marwah, two small mountains, and drink from the
Zamzam Well, a source of water believed to be provided by
Allah. Believers must stand vigil for an entire day at Mount
Arafat, the hill where Muhammad delivered his Farewell
Sermon, praying for Allah to forgive their sins and provide

personal strength. At sunset, pilgrims move to Muzdalifa, a flat plain where they collect 70 stones and sleep in tents or out in the open. The next day, they perform the symbolic stoning of the devil with the stones they have collected, flinging pebbles at three walls, which used to be pillars, called *jamaraat*, in the city of Mina. Following that ritual, they shave their heads, perform an animal sacrifice by slaughtering sheep, goats, camels, and cattle, and celebrate the festival of Eid al-Adha, the Islamic day of Sacrifice.

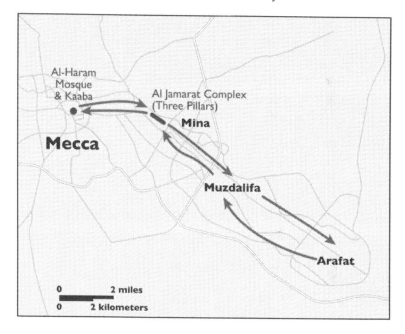

An annual gathering that attracts this many people is bound to be a logistical nightmare and a risky undertaking. The rapid increase in earth's human population coupled with the spread of Islam means there are more people than ever trying to attend the Hajj. Affordable jet travel now makes it easier for Muslims worldwide to attend. The result is that more and more people travel to Mecca, and officials must deal with the logistics of providing transportation, food, shelter, sanitation, and emergency services for millions of visitors at one time.

The Grand Mosque and the Ka'aba

The Ka'aba during the Hajj

Crowd control disasters have been commonplace in recent years. In 1990, in a pedestrian tunnel exiting Mecca toward Mina, 1,426 pilgrims died in a stampede. At least 270 pilgrims were killed in a stampede at the stoning of the devil ritual in 1994. In 1998, 118 were trampled to death on the Jamaraat Bridge in a panic after several people fell off the overpass. A stampede at the stoning of the devil ritual in 2001 killed 35. Fourteen more died in 2003. A stoning ritual stampede claimed another 251 lives in 2004, and 346 more in 2006, when an estimated two million pilgrims were taking part in the ritual. The stoning ritual is especially dangerous, because, being on the last day of the Hajj, many of the pilgrims drag their luggage behind them, creating a tripping and trampling risk, which was the cause of the 2006 stampede. Peddlers often block traffic, and pilgrims often ignore the directions for the entrance and exit ramps at the stoning ritual site. The 2006 stampede led to the reconstruction of the multilevel Jamaraat Bridge, which provides separate access and departure routes. Pre-determined schedules are now insisted upon by the Saudis to prevent overcrowding.

The tented field at Mina has also been the scene of repeated disasters. In 1975, 200 were killed in a fire after a cooking gas cylinder exploded. In 1997, 343 died and 1,500 were injured when fire swept through the tent city, again caused by exploding canisters of cooking gas. An estimated 40,000 tents were destroyed in the blaze, fanned by 40 mph (64 kph) winds; many of the dead were trampled in the ensuing panic. Unofficial sources claim more than 2,000 died. The replacement tents are now fireproof.

The multilevel Jamaraat Bridge in the foreground, where the stoning of the devil takes place, with the tent city of Mina in the background.

Violence has also broken out at the Hajj. In 1979, 200 to 500 militants calling for the overthrow of the Saudi government occupied the Grand Mosque. It took two weeks for the military to remove the insurgents; the death toll was 250, with 600 injured; 63 captured rebels were publicly beheaded after a secret trial. In 1987, Iranian pilgrims rioted when security forces sealed part of a route planned for an anti-American and anti-Israeli demonstration; the Saudis prohibit political activity during the Hajj, but Iranians continue to insist on holding rallies. In 1989, one pilgrim was killed and 16 injured when two bombings occurred.

A concrete hotel near the Grand Mosque collapsed during the 2006 Hajj; the official death toll stands at 76, with 64 injured. On September 11, 2015, ten days before the start of the 2015 Hajj, a construction crane collapsed through the roof of the Grand Mosque because of a severe sand and rain storm with high winds; 107 people inside the mosque were killed, and at least 238 injured.

The Grand Mosque is the largest in the world and surrounds the Ka'aba. It is being expanded to make the annual pilgrimage more manageable. Thirteen days after the crane collapse, on September 24, 2015 during the stoning ritual, another stampede on a street in the tent city in Mina killed more than 2,000. It was the deadliest Hajj incident to date, and one of the deadliest human crush disasters in history.

The mass of people visiting from various countries also has led to the spread of preventable infectious diseases. An international outbreak of meningitis followed the 1987 Hajj; Saudi officials now require specific vaccines in order to obtain a visa to take part in the Hajj. Middle East respiratory syndrome has been a concern in recent years. Hundreds also die each year from natural causes, as many pilgrims are older and have saved all their lives to be able to make the journey.

Despite these tragedies, the Saudis deserve credit for taking many successful steps to reduce the risk inherent in gatherings of millions of people. First-time visitors are preferred when issuing visas, and repeat visits are discouraged. Saudi Arabia sets quotas for individual countries to limit the number of foreign visitors. The Saudi government has spent more than $100 billion on improving pilgrimage facilities since the 1950s, and now provides much-improved facilities for housing, sanitation, and health care. An extensive system of bridges and structures have been built to move large masses of people more safely.

In recent years, a security force of more than 60,000 patrol the sites and deter attacks by religious extremists who wish to overthrow the Saudi government and its control of the holy city. Helicopters monitor the crowds from above, while security forces watch on closed-circuit television.

The Saudis have also changed rituals to be more symbolic, in order to ensure safety with the enormous number of people present. Now, pilgrims are not required to kiss the Black Stone, a stone set into the side of the Ka'aba, believed to have fallen from Heaven to show Adam and Eve where to build their altar, and set into the side of the Ka'aba by Muhammad. They can merely point to it as they pass by. Instead of the animal sacrifice ritual, pilgrims can purchase a voucher, which allows someone else to perform the sacrifice in their name.

After the 2004 Hajj, the three pillars at which pilgrims throw pebbles were rebuilt as long walls, surrounded by the Jamaraat Bridge, which allows more people to throw stones simultaneously from two levels. (Incidentally, when the *jamaraat* were pillars, pilgrims would inadvertently strike people on the other side of the pillar with their stones, resulting in injuries.) Over a few years after the January 2006 Hajj, the old bridge was demolished, and a new four-level bridge was constructed by the Bin Laden Group. The pillars were expanded to longer walls, more ramps and tunnels were built to make ingress and egress easier and safer, and the complex was re-engineered to avoid bottlenecks. The Saudis also issued a fatwa decreeing that the stoning of the devil may take place between sunrise and sunset, instead of right after the noon prayer, which had been tradition.

23

Italian Hall Disaster

1913

Michigan, USA

"The following listed persons died in a fire at the Italian Hall at Calumet and they were families of strikers who were celebrating Christmas. A stupid person yelled fire and caused a great panic." — Daily Mining Gazette, December 25, 1913

The Copper Country of Michigan's Upper Peninsula was the world's greatest producer of copper from the mid-1800s to the mid-1900s. The Western Federation of Miners had built up their membership by 1913 to call a strike against the Calumet and Hecla Mining Company (C&H). The union membership voted to demand that C&H recognize the union and convene a conference to discuss adjusting wages, hours, and working conditions. Company managers refused the request, and a strike was called on July 23, 1913.

The mines of the Upper Peninsula shut down immediately. In a time when unions were not protected by law, the mining companies called for the National Guard to be activated and hired hundreds of strike breakers. Soon, when it appeared there was nothing for them to do, the governor recalled the National Guard. The next day, strikebreakers shot and killed two strikers in broad daylight.

The strike would go on until April 1914; by Christmas 1913, it had been going on for five months. The Ladies Auxiliary of the Western Federation of Miners sponsored a

Christmas party for the striking miners and their families on Christmas Eve, December 24, 1913, at the Italian Hall in Calumet. More than 400 people gathered for the party on the second floor of the hall. A steep stairway was the only entrance to the hall, accessible by a double door at ground level. There was one poorly-marked emergency exit, and escape ladders on the back of the building, accessed only by climbing out the windows. The architects had included doors that swung outward, the latest in fire safety building features and a new building code established in the U.S. after the 1903 Iroquois Theater fire, the 1908 Collinwood School fire, and the 1911 Triangle Shirtwaist Factory fire.

At the celebration, children recited Christmas poems and sang carols. Santa Claus appeared to pass out presents. A man suddenly opened the door and yelled "Fire!" while Christmas presents were being distributed; despite attempts by some in the crowd to detain him, he escaped down the stairs. The panicked crowd rushed for the stairs, and 73 people, 59 of them children, were crushed in the stampede. Eight witnesses testified under oath that the person who yelled "Fire!" was a member of the Citizen's Alliance, an organization that was anti-union and supported the mine owners during labor strikes. It has been suggested that the purpose of the cry was to disrupt the party and discredit the union. No witnesses ever reported an actual fire; the local volunteer fire department's log book from that Christmas Eve states there was no fire.

Rescuers quickly arrived, only to find a mass of tangled people blocking the entrance. Responders had to climb up the ladders and through the windows to pull survivors and victims from the mass of bodies. The deepest mass of victims was at the bottom of the stairs; apparently the surging crowd had knocked the first people to reach the stairs to the bottom, where they were trampled and suffocated. The bodies quickly piled up.

Charles Moyer, the president of the Western Federation of Miners, publicly announced that an agent of the Citizen's Alliance had yelled "Fire!" and the organization was responsible for the disaster. Shortly thereafter, in nearby Hancock and in view of the local sheriff, Moyer was assaulted, shot, and kidnapped; he was placed on a train and told never to return to Michigan. Instead, Moyer received medical attention in Chicago, held a press conference and showed his gunshot wound, and returned to Upper Michigan to rally for the strikers.

In 1984, the Italian Hall was demolished, but the original archway that led upstairs to the disaster scene remains; a state historical marker provides details of the disaster at the site, which is now managed by the Keweenaw National Historical Park.

The Italian Hall, the day after the disaster,
and all that remains of the building today.

24

LeMans Crash

1955

France

On June 11, 1955, a crowd of about 250,000 gathered for 24 Hours of LeMans in France. The race followed an 8.38-mile (13.5-km) circuit. Of the 70 cars that arrived for the event, the top 60 were selected to compete.

Forty-nine-year-old Pierre Levegh of France was hired by Mercedes-Benz to drive their entry in the race. Levegh had impressed Mercedes-Benz in 1952 by driving for 23 hours straight without relief from a replacement driver.

Mercedes-Benz had racing success with its new sports car, the 300 SLR, in 1955. The 300 SLR developed 310 horsepower with a 2,982-cc engine, but weighed only 2,457 pounds (1,114 kg). The car's body was made from an ultralight magnesium alloy, reducing vehicle weight and therefore improving performance. The car, however, still used a traditional drum brake system; some of the rival race cars had new state-of-the-art disc brakes. To compensate, engineers installed a large air brake to quickly slow the vehicle as it entered turns.

The race cars lacked seat belts; drivers preferred to be thrown clear of a wreck rather than be trapped in a burning vehicle.

The LeMans circuit had remained essentially unchanged since the first LeMans race in 1923. In that time, top speeds of the race cars had increased from 62 mph (100 kph) to 190 mph (300 kph). Safety measures to protect the public were inadequate; spectators along the straightaway near the grandstand were protected by only a chest-high berm and a picket fence. Levegh had complained about the LeMans course, saying the cars now moved too fast for it.

Two hours into the 24-hour race, on lap 35, Mike Hawthorn of Great Britain, driving a Jaguar D-type race car, noticed a signal to enter the pit for refueling. He braked his car quickly to enter the pit, using his new disc brakes. The sudden movement caused Lance Macklin of Great Britian, driving an older Austin-Healy 100, to brake hard; the action threw up a cloud of dust, blinding Levegh, who was following close behind. Macklin swerved out of control across the track; Levegh did not have time to react, and he struck Macklin's car while traveling at about 150 mph (240 kph).

Levegh's car became airborne and landed on the earthen embankment on the left side of track, which served to separate spectators from the race track. It launched into a series of somersaults for about 85 yards (78 m), causing parts of the car to fly apart at high speed. The hood separated from the car and flew into the crowd, decapitating many of the spectators before they could react. The front axle and the engine block likewise sailed into the crowd.

The rear-mounted fuel tank ruptured and burst into flames, igniting the car's body with its high magnesium content. Magnesium is a highly flammable metal. It continues to burn at a high temperature when nitrogen, carbon dioxide, or even water are applied, making a magnesium fire difficult to extinguish once is has been ignited. The suddenly-flaming car body sent white-hot burning embers into the crowd.

Macklin's car had struck the pit wall on the right of the track in the chaos. It then crossed the track again and struck the embankment near the burning Mercedes-Benz, killing a spectator. Macklin escaped serious injury.

As the Mercedez-Benz disintegrates, its hood and front axle can be seen sailing into the crowd of spectators.

Hawthorn missed the pit entrance and continued around the circuit for one more lap before pulling in for his relief driver. He reportedly had tears streaming down his face when he got out of his car and could see the chaos on the other side of the course.

Levegh had been thrown clear of the somersaulting car, but he suffered from a crushed skull when he landed and did not survive. Rescue workers, unfamiliar with magnesium fires, poured water on the fire. This only intensified the blaze, sending white-hot balls of fire surging into the crowd. The car burned for hours.

The 1955 LeMans disaster resulted in the deaths of Pierre Levegh and 83 spectators, with more than 120 injured. It was the worst accident in motorsports history. Vivid newsreel footage of the disaster can be seen on YouTube at https://www.youtube.com/watch?v=RMoh5hZAaZk&feature=channel_video_title.

Minutes after the crash, the Mercedes-Benz burns near a spectator who had just perished.

The race continued, in part to prevent the departing crowd from clogging the roads and blocking emergency vehicles. Daimler-Benz, the maker of the Mercedes-Benz brand, withdrew their entries (which were in the two leading positions) out of respect for the victims about eight hours after the crash, but others kept going until the race finished the next day. Mike Hawthorn, whose sudden braking had set off the chain reaction that caused the disaster, finished in first place in record time.

The official investigation into the disaster determined that the crash was an accident. The spectators' deaths, however, were blamed on inadequate safety standards and track design. The disaster led to the ban of motorsports in a number of countries, including France, Spain, Switzerland, and Germany, until tracks could be improved to better protect spectators. Switzerland's prohibition on motor racing continues to this day; parliament in 2003 and 2009 decided not to overturn the ban. A number of car manufacturers, including Daimler-Benz, soon pulled out of motorsports competitions, focusing instead on building the vehicles that others would use in motor racing. At LeMans, the Grandstand and pit areas were taken down, redesigned, and rebuilt soon after the disaster.

Levegh's co-driver, American John Fitch, tried to convince Daimler-Benz management to pull out of the race several times in the hours after the crash. The German team was now involved in the worst racing accident ever on French soil, and it was only ten years after the end of the German occupation of France in World War II. Fitch believed there was only one thing to do. He finally succeeded after eight hours. Fitch spent the rest of his career advocating for safety improvements for vehicles, drivers, and motorsports spectators.

Two hours after the crash, priests walk among the dead, to whom they had administered last rites.

25

Goiânia Radioactive Contamination Accident

1987

Brazil

"They had no idea what it was. People saw the light of the cesium and thought it was a precious gem," — Manoel Ramos, 26, technician for Brazil's Nuclear Energy Commission

In 1985, The Instituto Goiano de Radioterapia (IGR) in Goiânia, Brazil, the capital of the state of Goiás, moved to a new location in the city of over a million people. IGR was a private radiotherapy clinic. IGR and the owner of the property, the Society of Saint Vincent de Paul, fell into a court dispute over the removal of equipment that was left behind. One of these pieces of equipment was a teletherapy unit that contained about 3.3 ounces (93 grams) of highly radioactive caesium chloride inside a canister made of lead and steel.

The abandoned building had large holes in the walls, where adjoining facilities had been demolished; it was completely open and accessible to the public. Indeed, there was evidence that it was being used by the homeless. On May 4, 1987, one of the owners of IGR, Carlos Figueiredo Bezerril, attempted to remove some objects which had been left behind at the abandoned hospital, including the caesium canister. He was stopped by police. Figueiredo subsequently warned authorities about the canister. The court responded by posting a security guard on-site to protect the equipment.

The owners of IGR wrote several letters to Brazil's National Nuclear Energy Commission, warning them about the presence of radiological equipment at the site. However, a court order prevented anyone from removing the dangerous materials.

On September 13, 1987, two scrap collectors, Roberto dos Santos Alves and Wagner Mota Pereira, entered the abandoned building while the guard was absent from his post. They disassembled the teletherapy unit, hoping to find parts with some scrap value. They took the canister of caesium home in a wheelbarrow; there, they began to take the equipment apart.

That evening, both of the scavengers began to vomit; however, they continued to dismantle the stolen equipment. By the next day, Pereira's left hand began to swell, and he was suffering from dizziness and diarrhea. Soon a burn was noticeable on his left hand, in the same size and shape as the aperture on the canister. On September 15, a local clinic diagnosed his symptoms as having come from something he ate; he was sent home to rest.

Alves continued to dismantle the radiological equipment. He was able to free the caesium capsule from the canister. On September 16, he punctured the canister's aperture window with a screwdriver and could see a deep blue light emanating from within. He scooped some of the glowing substance out with the screwdriver. He tried to light it on fire, believing it was some sort of gunpowder, but it would not ignite. A friend of his took a rice-sized piece and put it in his front pocket, intending to take it home and use it in a ring for his wife. The substance burned through his pants, causing serious radiation burns. His wife, suspecting the substance was the cause of his sudden vomiting, diarrhea, and burns, took the substance and flushed it down the toilet. She suffered from burns on her fingers.

Two days later (September 18), Alves sold the objects to a scrapyard. Devair Alves Ferreira, the owner of the scrapyard, noticed later that night the blue glow from the canister. He took it into his house, convinced that the object was valuable and perhaps supernatural. For three days, he invited friends and family to his house to see it. He paid about $25 for the cylinder, and wanted to make a ring for his wife from the glowing substance and pieces of the metal cylinder. He stored the cylinder in his wife's clothes closet for safekeeping.

On September 21, one of Ferreira's friends managed to scoop out several rice-sized pieces of the glowing material using a screwdriver. Ferreira shared them with friends and family. That same day his wife, Gabriela Maria Ferreira, became ill. One of Ferreira's brothers used the substance to make a cross on his abdomen.

On September 24, Ferreira's brother Ivo scraped more of the material out of the canister and took it home. He spread it on the cement floor. His six-year-old daughter, Leide das Neves Ferreira, sat on the floor and ate a sandwich. Fascinated with the glowing substance, she spread it on her body and showed it to her mother. Dust from the glowing material fell on the sandwich she was eating.

The next day, Ferreira sold the canister and the glowing material to another scrapyard.

On September 28, Gabriela Maria Ferreira managed to track down the material and took it to a hospital in a plastic bag for examination. Neighbors believed the Ferreiras' symptoms were from AIDS. She was examined at the Center of Information on Toxic Drugs. The next day, a local physicist confirmed the presence of radioactivity and notified the authorities, who were persuaded to take action. The local, state, and national governments were all aware of the situation by the end of the day. Gabriela Maria Ferreira's actions probably saved many lives.

News of the contamination spread quickly in the media. The media and the general population compared the situation to Chernobyl, which had occurred the year before. Within a few days, almost 130,000 people feared they had been exposed. Of those people, 249 tested positive for radioactive residue on their skin; 20 people showed signs of radiation sickness and received treatment. At the Ferreira junkyard, 23 chickens, five pigs, two rabbits, and two dogs were contaminated and had to be destroyed.

There were four deaths related to the incident. Six-year-old Leide das Neves Ferreira, who had sat on the floor and spread the radiological substance on her body, suffered from swelling, hair loss, kidney and lung damage, and internal bleeding. She was confined to an isolation room at a hospital in Rio de Janeiro because the staff was afraid of contaminating themselves. An international team arrived to care for her, but she died on October 23. A special fiberglass coffin lined with lead was built for her burial, but the news of her impending burial in the local cemetery in Goiânia caused more than 2,000 people to riot, fearing her corpse would contaminate the community. Although the protesters tried to pile stones and bricks in the road leading into the cemetery to prevent the burial, they were not successful in stopping it.

Gabriela Maria Ferreira, 37, wife of the junkyard owner, was sick within three days of coming in contact with the substance. She developed internal bleeding, and suffered from hair loss. She also died on October 23.

Admilson Alves de Souza, 18, and Israel Baptista dos Santos, 22, were employees of Devair Ferreira who had worked to disassemble the equipment at the junkyard. They both developed radiation sickness and died on October 18 and 27, respectively.

Pereira, who had dismantled the canister with the radiological substance inside, eventually had to have several fingers on his left hand partially amputated. Alves, the other scavenger, had his right forearm amputated. Devair Ferreira survived a massive dose of radiation; he subsequently suffered from depression and died in 1994 from binge drinking. Survivors still report that, decades after the incident, they are still treated with suspicion and prejudice.

The original capsule that held the substance was seized by the Brazilian military as soon as they became aware of the situation. Since then, the capsule has been on display at the School of Specialized Instruction in Rio de Janeiro.

Three doctors who owned and ran IGR were charged with criminal negligence. The two scrap dealers who had stolen the equipment were not charged. One of the owners of IGR and the company's physicist were ordered to pay a fine for the derelict condition of the building. In 2000, a federal court ordered the National Nuclear Energy Commission to pay R$1.3 million (nearly US$750,000) for medical and psychological treatment for direct and indirect victims of the contamination, and their descendants for three generations.

To clean up the mess, at least 14 contaminated sites were identified. Workers who arrived in Goiânia to clean up the contamination did not come with protective clothing, so they purchased white coveralls and tennis shoes from a local store. Topsoil was removed from several sites, and several houses were demolished. The contents of those houses were examined, and those objects with radiological contamination were decontaminated or taken away as contaminated waste. Cleanup was hampered because the canister had been compromised and radiological particles were spread throughout the area. The workers became contaminated themselves because of the lack of protective gear.

The root cause of the incident was the lack of adequate accounting procedures for radioactive materials in Brazil. The National Nuclear Energy Commission, which was closely tied with the Brazilian military, was responsible for both establishing and implementing procedures, as well as promoting the nuclear industry.

The Goiânia incident has been studied in preparation for developing procedures to deal with the possible detonation of a "dirty bomb," which would release radiological material into the air. The Goiânia incident has been compared to a medium-sized dirty bomb; thousands or tens of thousands would fear contamination, but in reality only a few hundred might be actually contaminated, and a few dozen severely enough to require medical treatment.

26

Saint-Michel-de-Maurienne Derailment

1917

France

During times of war in the 20th century, railways played an important role in moving troops and supplies to and from the front lines. Military use of rail lines and equipment took precedence over civilian use, and equipment and the men needed to maintain and operate it was in short supply. Old, improperly maintained equipment was often used, and trains were often loaded beyond capacity.

In the midst of World War I, on December 12, 1917, nearly 1,000 French troops were granted leave for 15 days to visit family during the holidays. (Incidentally, it was only six days after the explosion that leveled Halifax, Nova Scotia.) Fighting on the front in northeastern Italy, they boarded an Italian train back to France. Two trains were coupled together; the train was made of 19 cars, two of which were baggage cars. The train weighed approximately 580 tons (526 metric tons) and was more than 383 yards (350 meters) long; the cars were constructed of wood on a metal chassis. The train carried 982 enlisted soldiers.

Normally, a train of this size would have two locomotives. However, the second locomotive was requisitioned for another train carrying munitions, leaving one locomotive for the troop train. The first three coaches had air brakes; the remaining coaches only had hand brakes, or no brakes at all. The train was four times the size deemed safe for the braking system.

The rail line passed through Modane and Saint Michel de Maurienne. The stretch between the two stations was a steep 3.3% downhill grade, and passed through the narrow Maurienne Valley, where the speed limit was 25 mph (40 kph). The engineer knew the route well, and refused to take the severely overloaded train down the incline. The commanding officer for rail traffic threatened military discipline, and the engineer was forced to proceed. Seven brakemen were distributed throughout the train; they would apply the hand brakes on the coaches when the locomotive whistle blew.

After waiting at the Modane station for an hour to let other trains pass, the train departed at 11:15 p.m. As the train descended into the valley, the engineer applied the brakes, but they had no effect. Soon the train accelerated to an uncontrollable speed; it eventually reached 84 mph (135 kph) on the steepest section of the line. After traveling about 4 miles (6.5 km) and shortly before the Saint Michel de Maurienne station, where it was traveling at 60 mph (102 kph), the first coach derailed. The rest of the coaches telescoped into one another and burst into flames.

The electrical system on the Italian train was not operating at the time of the derailment; the fire was blamed on candles being used for lighting. To make matters worse, some of the soldiers were carrying grenades and other munitions home, without authorization. Exploding munitions compounded the fire and loss of life. The fire continued to burn until the following night.

Along the route, the station master at La Praz had watched the train hurtle downhill past the station. He notified the station master at Saint Jean de Maurienne, who held a train full of British soldiers, ready to depart uphill into the disaster scene. This prevented an even greater disaster from taking place.

The engineer, too busy dealing with the failed brakes, did not notice the rest of the train had derailed. Because of the decoupling of most of the train, and the loss of the excess weight, he was able to stop the locomotive and its tender at the Saint Jean de Maurienne station, where he realized what had happened. He headed back to the accident site with Scottish soldiers waiting for a train in the opposite direction. There, they found that the inferno, the height of the piled-up wreckage, and the narrow, rocky terrain made it difficult to assist the survivors.

The military hospital in Saint Jean de Maurienne and a nearby paté factory were transformed into makeshift field hospitals and morgues.

About 700 soldiers died in the disaster. Because many were burned beyond recognition, only 425 could be identified. Thirty-seven of the bodies were strewn along the tracks uphill from the accident scene; they had either been thrown from the jostling train, or had jumped off the train as it hurtled out of control down into the valley. More than 100 of the deaths occurred during transport to or at the hospital. Only 183 soldiers reported for roll call the next morning.

It was the worst rail disaster in French history, and remained a classified military secret for years. The French government enforced a ban on any detailed reporting of the catastrophe.

Six employees of the railway, PLM (Paris–Lyon–Mediterranée) Railway, were tried in a court-martial, but were acquitted.

27

Bhopal Gas Leak

1984

India

"While driving down to this hospital — actually it's a hospital plus an educational institute where they train doctors — so on the way we found dead animals, bloated bodies and people rushing and it was very chaotic. And when we got there it was like the war had just ended or an earthquake had just finished and people were trying to recover their dead and wounded ones." —Raghu Rai, photographer sent to Bhopal to document the aftereffects

A Union Carbide Corporation (UCC) chemical plant on the outskirts of Bhopal, Madhya Pradesh, India, was the scene of the world's worst industrial accident. A gas leak at the plant on the night of December 2–3, 1984, exposed 700,000 people to methyl isocyanate (MIC) gas, as well as other caustic chemicals.

The chemical plant, built in 1969, used MIC to produce pesticides. The pesticide Sevin was manufactured there; at the time, it was considered to be the environmentally-preferred alternative to DDT. Several MIC leaks occurred inside the plant between 1976 and 1984, injuring dozens of workers and causing one death. By November 1984, the aging plant was falling into disrepair. Many valves and lines were in poor condition. Most of the safety systems no longer functioned; the same was true of the vent gas scrubbers and the steam boiler, which were used to clean pipes.

Tank 610 contained 42 tons of MIC, which was more than safety protocols allowed. On the night of December 2, water entered the tank through a side pipe, causing a runaway chemical reaction. The reaction was accelerated by the presence of contaminants, such as iron from rusting pipelines, and from high temperatures. The temperature inside the tank surpassed 392°F (200°C), raising the pressure and resulting in an emergency venting from the tank of MIC. A large volume of toxic gases (33 tons, 30 metric tons) was released into the air over the next hour.

The toxic gas cloud was mainly composed of chemicals that were more dense than the surrounding air, so the gas cloud flowed near the ground as it spread outwards from the plant. The plant was surrounded by shanty towns in which hundreds of thousands of people lived.

Nearby residents awoke to coughing, irritated eyes, burning respiratory tracts, the inability to breathe, and stomach pains and vomiting. They attempted to flee from the plant, but by running they inhaled more toxic gases. Because the gas cloud was thickest near the ground, shorter people and children inhaled more of the gases.

Thousands were dead by morning. Hundreds of thousands suffered the effects of inhaling poisonous gases, and the local health care system was quickly overloaded. At least 200,000 children had been exposed. Most medical staff in Bhopal was not trained in proper procedures for treating MIC gas inhalation.

Mass funerals were held and many of the victims were quickly cremated. At least 170,000 people were treated at local hospitals and clinics. The official death toll immediately after the disaster was 2,259, but rose to 3,787 according to the state government. The Indian government reported 558,125 injured, with 3,900 of those injuries severe and permanently disabling. Other reports claim 8,000 deaths within two weeks and another 8,000 dead since then from diseases related to inhaling the gas.

Trees in the area around the plant lost their leaves within a few days. Thousands of buffalo, goats, and other animal carcasses needed to be buried. Food supplies in the area dwindled, as no one wanted to enter the disaster zone to make deliveries. Fish in local waterways were found to be contaminated, so that source of food was also eliminated from the local diet.

On December 16, two tanks at the plant were emptied of the remaining MIC by the only feasible way: to reactivate the plant and continue the pesticide manufacturing process. The area was evacuated of residents to prevent another disaster.

But what had really caused the water to enter the tank and start the chemical reaction which led to the accident? There are two working theories, neither one proven more than 30 years later. Both corporate negligence and worker sabotage have been blamed.

Union Carbide has been accused of corporate negligence, which led to the disaster: a lack of safety features leading to a dangerous working environment, a total lack of emergency plans in case of catastrophe, filling tanks over capacity, poor maintenance, and turning off safety systems to save money (the MIC tank refrigeration unit, which would have reduced the amount of gas released, had been shut down). Investigations uncovered that management and workers were unskilled in proper procedures, and the company cut costs by underinvesting in plant safety. There were communication problems and cross-cultural barriers between Union Carbide and its Indian operator, Union Carbide India Limited (UCIL). Operations manuals were in

English, although few of the workers had a grasp of the English language. Local authorities were never informed of what was being manufactured at the plant, what might happen should a malfunction at the plant take place, or what should be done about it.

By 1984, the use of MIC in producing pesticides was decreasing, so safety practices had deteriorated along with the number of trained staff assigned to the process. Employee morale was low; workers' complaints to their unions about safety and training issues were ignored.

In the company investigation after the disaster, Union Carbide admitted that most of the plant's safety systems were not operating that night. The MIC tank alarms that would have warned of an impending problem had been inoperable for four years. Only one gas scrubber was in working condition, and it could not handle the amount of gas building up in the tank; the others had been out of service for five months. The flare tower, which could only handle a quarter of the gas that had built up, wasn't even working that night. To save refrigeration costs, the MIC was kept at 68°F (20°C), not the 40°F (4.5°C) the operations manual indicated. A UCC internal report in September 1984, a few months before the Bhopal incident, looked at a similarly designed plant in Virginia, and found numerous defects and malfunctions. The report warned that "a runaway reaction could occur in the MIC unit storage tanks, and that the planned response would not be timely or effective enough to prevent catastrophic failure of the tanks." The report was not forwarded to the Bhopal plant.

According to this theory, the direct cause of the gas release, the intrusion of water into the tank, was the result of workers using water to clean nearby pipes. The water entered the tank due to improper maintenance of the clogged and leaky pipes. This negligence theory, however, has some holes. An analysis indicates the pipes being cleaned were far too small to produce enough hydraulic pressure for the water to flow into the tank at the rate it did. A key valve would have had to be open for this to occur, and inspections confirmed it was indeed closed at the time. Also, the pipes would still have been filled with water after the disaster, as there was no drain, but they were found to be dry by inspectors after the accident.

For these reasons, Union Carbide, now owned by Dow Chemical Company, claims that the accident was the result of worker sabotage. This same analysis by Arthur D. Little concluded that a single disgruntled employee, without detection, deliberately pumped water into the tank to contaminate its contents. Multiple witnesses reported that, immediately after the accident, the pressure indicator was missing from Tank 610, and next to the open pipe was a hose with water running out of it. Logs had been falsified or even destroyed. Immediately before the gas release, an attempt was made to transfer one ton of water out of the tank, but, after the gas release, the logs were falsified to cover up the failed attempt. MIC operators claimed that water had entered through a hose connected to the pipe at the missing pressure gauge.

Little claims that the following took place: At 10:20, the tank pressure was normal. At 10:45, there was a shift change, during which the MIC tank area would be deserted. During the shift change, "a disgruntled operator entered the storage area and hooked up one of the readily available rubber water hoses to Tank 610, with the intention of contaminating and spoiling the tank's contents." Water began to flow into the tank and the runaway reaction began. After midnight, control room operators realized the pressure was building up in the tank; the supervisor decided to investigate after tea, which lasted until 12:45. At that time, workers reportedly went to the tank, found it rumbling, with the concrete around the tank cracking. They discovered the hose pumping water into the tank and tried to pump out some of its contents. Before they could accomplish that, the gas was released. The workers then began to cover up what had happened. UCC insists that the safety measures in place and operational at the time would prevent that much water from entering the tank by accident, so "employee sabotage—not faulty design or operation—was the cause of the tragedy."

Victims did receive ongoing compensation after the disaster. Shortly after the accident, widows received a pension of $3.20 per month, later raised to $12. Families with less than $7.90 in monthly income received a $24 monthly payment. By October 2003, 554,985 people had received compensation for injuries, and 15,310 received benefits as survivors of those killed. The average death benefit was $2,200, and the injured received on average $400. In 2007, courts set the number of injured receiving benefits at 574,304; total compensation at this point was $250 million. In 2010, another aid package was awarded by the Indian government for $200 million.

Union Carbide, while insisting that a worker had sabotaged the plant, did provide relief operations and funding from the start. The day after the gas leak, the company sent aid and a medical team to Bhopal. Within days, it had transferred $2 million to the government disaster relief fund. At least $9.6 million was added to relief funds over the next several years. The company also funded the construction and ongoing operation of a hospital in the neighborhood to treat the victims of the disaster.

Union Carbide settled with the Supreme Court of India in 1989 and immediately paid $470 million to the Indian government to pay for relief. Statements by both Union Carbide and the Supreme Court admitted that the amount was far greater than what would normally be payable under Indian law.

The first criminal convictions took place in June 2010, when eight ex-employees of UCIL, including the former UCIL chairman, were sentenced to two years and fined about $2,000 each for causing death by negligence.

28

Kyshtym Nuclear Disaster

1957

USSR/Russia

"About 100 kilometres from Sverdlovsk, a highway sign warned drivers not to stop for the next 20 or 30 kilometres and to drive through at maximum speed. On both sides of the road, as far as one could see, the land was dead: no villages, no towns, only the chimneys of destroyed houses, no cultivated fields or pastures, no herds, no people...nothing." —Lev Tumerman, Soviet scientist, confirming Medvedev's account in 1960

At the end of World War II, the United States was the world's only nuclear power. The Soviet Union quickly established a research and development program to produce weapons-grade uranium and plutonium and strike a military balance with the world's only other superpower. Soviet physicists did not yet understand all there was to know about nuclear physics, and some environmental and safety decisions were made which proved later to be disastrous.

A plutonium production site and nuclear fuel reprocessing plant was built at Mayak between 1945 and 1948, near the town of Kyshtym in the southern Ural Mountains. The area had long been used for munitions production. It was the first plant to create plutonium for the Soviet nuclear program, and became the largest nuclear complex in the world. Six reactors were built on the shores of Lake Kyzyltash and Lake Karachay. Lake Kyzyltash, the larger lake, provided water for cooling; Lake Karachay was a convenient place to dump the radioactive waste. Their cooling systems discharged contaminated water directly back into the lakes. High level radioactive waste was also eventually dumped into the Techa River, which emptied into the Arctic Ocean.

In 1953, a storage facility for liquid nuclear waste was built at Mayak; it was made of steel tanks within a concrete base 27 feet (8.2 m) underground. The waste was soon heating itself because of the high level of radioactivity, so a cooling system was constructed around the tanks. However, the tanks and their cooling system were inadequately monitored by plant operators.

The cooling system in one of the tanks failed on September 29, 1957. Nearly 80 tons (72.5 metric tons) of liquid radioactive waste was stored in the tank at the time. The temperature inside the tank quickly rose, and the waste, mostly ammonium nitrate and acetates, exploded. The blast, estimated at 70–100 tons (63–91 metric tons) of TNT, threw the 160-ton (145-metric ton) concrete tank lid into the air.

Ammonium nitrate was the key ingredient in a number of large-scale explosions, some intentional and some not, through history, including the 1947 Texas City explosion (chapter 39), the 1993 World Trade Center bombing, the 1995 Oklahoma City federal building bombing, and the 2013 West Fertilizer Company explosion in West, Texas.

Although no one died in the explosion, radioactive contamination settled in the area around the plant, and a plume of radioactive material spread hundreds of miles/kilometers from the plant. The Techa River and Lake Karachay were further contaminated. Over the next 11 hours, the radioactive plume spread northeast 190–220 miles (300–350 km). The fallout contaminated as much as 7,700 square miles (20,000 square kilometers) with caesium-137 and strontium-90. This area is now called the East-Ural Radioactive Trace (EURT).

About 10,000 people from 22 villages were evacuated from the fallout zone; some were evacuated a week later, but others were evacuated as long as two years later. Because the Soviets kept all information about their nuclear program a secret, the local population was not informed for a week, and even then were given no explanation of the dangers. Residents continued to drink water from local rivers and eat food grown locally.

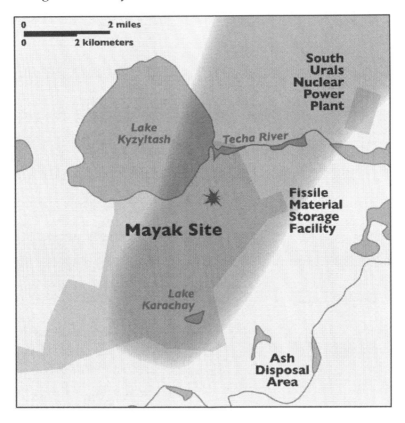

By April 1958, the western press was getting wind of some catastrophic accident creating radioactive fallout. Over the next couple of decades, there were reports of some mysterious disease in the disaster zone, causing people's skin to slough off. The local population claimed the Soviet-controlled media reported that the Americans had poisoned the area, and the poison was spread when it rained. In 1976, Zhores Medvedev, a Russian biologist, historian, and dissident, succeeded in exposing the Kyshtym disaster. He published details in his book *The Nuclear Disaster in the Urals* in 1979 (W.W. Norton, New York). Medvedev was subsequently confined to a mental institution by the Soviet government, as was often done with dissidents in the communist state. His details of the disaster were derided by the western nuclear industry, but the accident and contamination were soon confirmed by other scientists.

In an attempt to contain the contamination, soil was excavated and stored in fenced enclosures. Scores of contaminated villages were apparently burned to the ground so that locals could not return; the fires spread more radioactive material over the area and further contaminated the food chain. In 1968, the Soviets attempted to disguise the EURT contaminated area by creating the East-Ural Nature Reserve and prohibiting any unauthorized access. The area remains devoid of human activity to this day. The Soviet Union began to declassify relevant documents in 1989.

Subsequent information released through the Freedom of Information Act in the U.S. reveals that the CIA knew of the Kyshtym disaster in 1959, but kept it secret so as not to adversely affect the American nuclear industry.

It is difficult to determine the number of deaths from the fallout plume at Kyshtym. Radiation-induced cancers are clinically indistinguishable from other cancers, so studies have been undertaken to determine the expected cancer death rate in the area, and compare it to the actual death rate. Estimates range from a few dozen deaths to more than

8,000, but the most commonly quoted estimate is about 200. Near the accident site, there were 66 diagnosed cases of chronic radiation syndrome.

The Kyshtym disaster measured as a Level 6 disaster on the International Nuclear Event Scale. Only two accidents have been worse: Chernobyl (1986, see Chapter 49) and Fukushima Daiichi (2011); both registered a seven, the highest number, on the scale.

The area of the EURT remains heavily contaminated to this day. Lake Karachay is still the most polluted place on earth, more so than around Chernobyl. The sediment at the bottom of the lake is almost entirely composed of high level radioactive waste 11 feet (3.4 m) thick. In 1990, it was estimated that the lake could give a lethal dose of radioactivity to a human within an hour. In 1967, a drought reduced the size of the lake and radioactive dust was blown from the dry portion of the lake; more than 400,000 people were irradiated.

At least 32 other serious nuclear accidents have occurred at Mayak, including at least four since 2000. The Russian government is reportedly considering importing nuclear waste to the Mayak site from all over the world.

29

SS *Eastland* Capsizing

1915

Illinois, USA

"And then movement caught my eye. I looked across the river. As I watched in disoriented stupefaction a steamer large as an ocean liner slowly turned over on its side as though it were a whale going to take a nap. I didn't believe a huge steamer had done this before my eyes, lashed to a dock, in perfectly calm water, in excellent weather, with no explosion, no fire, nothing. I thought I had gone crazy." —Jack Woodford, writer and witness, as printed in the *Herald and Examiner*

The USS *Eastland* was built in 1903 in Port Huron, Michigan, as a passenger ship. It was used as a tour vessel based in Chicago. Crew and passengers soon noticed that the vessel had a tendency to list to the side when passengers gathered on the upper decks, due to a center of gravity that was too high. In July 1904, the vessel severely listed at 20–25 degrees off the shore of South Haven, Michigan, when an over-capacity crowd of more than 3,000 congregated on the top deck. The ship was righted when the passengers were moved and the ballast tanks adjusted. Another severe listing occurred in 1906, when 2,530 passengers were aboard.

Following the RMS *Titanic* disaster in 1912, the Seamen's Act required passenger ships to be retrofitted to carry enough lifeboats for all passengers. Ironically, the addition of more lifeboats exacerbated the problem of the *Eastland* being top-heavy. Shipbuilders had opposed the new regulations, stating that some ships on the Great Lakes would become too top-heavy and prone to capsizing. The *Eastland* was given special restrictions regarding the number of passengers who could be allowed onboard: a maximum of 2,500.

On Saturday, July 24, 1915, the *Eastland* and four other passenger steamers were hired by the Western Electric Company's Hawthorne Works in Cicero, Illinois, to take employees to a picnic in Michigan City, Indiana. Most of the workers were unable to afford vacations, so this was a big deal to them.

Steamship inspectors were persuaded to raise the passenger capacity for the picnic excursion to make up for a dismal tourist season that year.

The *Eastland* was tied to the shore on the south side of the Chicago River between Clark and LaSalle Streets; it was only three blocks from the former Iroquois Theatre, which had burned a dozen years earlier with a tragic loss of life (see Chapter 3). Boarding began at 6:30 a.m., and by 7:10 she had reached her capacity of 2,572 passengers. Many of the passengers stood on the open upper decks, and the ship began to list to port, away from the riverbank. The crew pumped water into its ballast tanks to right the ship, but it made little difference. Within 15 minutes, many of the passengers rushed to the port side, and at 7:28 the ship suddenly rolled onto its side and came to rest on the river bottom, which was only 20 feet (6 m) under the surface.

Before the capsizing, many of the passengers, mostly women and children, had moved below decks because of cool, damp weather. They were trapped inside the ship as it rolled over; many of them were crushed by heavy furniture, such as pianos and tables.

Many of those on the upper decks were tossed into the river or stranded on the hull of the rolled ship, awaiting rescue. Some were trapped under the ship. A nearby ship, the *Kenosha*, quickly came alongside so that those stranded passengers could leap aboard. Despite the fact that the *Eastland* was only 20 feet (6 m) from the wharf, and despite the presence of the *Kenosha*, 841 passengers, two crew members, and one rescuer were killed.

Rescuers on the Eastland *as seen from the south side of the river shortly after the accident. Crowds line the river bank to watch the rescue operations.*

It was the largest loss of life from a single shipwreck on the Great Lakes. Twenty-two entire families had perished. Seventy percent of the victims were under the age of 25. The death toll among passengers was worse than on the *Titanic*, when 829 passengers, in addition to 694 crew members, were lost.

By 8:00 all survivors had been pulled from the river. Rescuers began to cut holes in the hull to rescue those trapped inside, but by then, most of them had drowned.

Recovered bodies were taken to a number of makeshift morgues set up to deal with the high number of casualties. Identification of bodies was difficult as passengers were not assigned to any particular ship, and there was no record made of names as passengers boarded the ships. Unidentified bodies were taken to the 2nd Regiment Armory, later the site of Harpo Studios and the sound stage for the *Oprah Winfrey Show.*

George Halas, who worked at the Western Electric Company and would one day help found the National Football League and coach the Chicago Bears, had a ticket for the ill-fated passage but arrived at the wharf too late to board the *Eastland.*

The first known film footage of rescue operations was discovered by a graduate student at the University of Chicago in 2015, and can be viewed at http://www. chicagotribune.com/news/daywatch/chi-eastland-disaster-film-footage-20150208-htmlstory.html.

The Eastland *as seen from a fire tug on the Chicago River.*
The Eastland *rests on its side on the river bottom, while bodies*
continue to be recovered.

The president and three other officers of the steamship company which owned the *Eastland* were indicted by a grand jury for manslaughter, and the ship's captain and engineer were charged with criminal carelessness. The grand jury ruled that the disaster was the result of ship instability caused by overloading, mishandling water ballast, and/or defective design.

Extradition hearings were held to return the indicted men to Illinois from Michigan. At the hearing, Sidney Jenks, the head of the shipbuilding company that had constructed the ship, testified that the original owners had wanted a fast ship that could transport fruit, so the *Eastland* had been designed to travel at 20 mph (32 kph) and carry 500 passengers. The ship was later converted to a passenger steamer with a capacity of more than 2,500 passengers. Jenks testified that there was never an actual stability test of the ship, but that upon launching, it listed at an angle of 45 degrees and then righted itself immediately, demonstrating its stability.

The court refused to pursue extradition, stating that the four company officers weren't even on the ship, the ship's officers had done everything by the books, and because the ship had proven seaworthy for years, there was no reason for anyone to think differently.

Litigation continued for 20 years, but no one was ever held accountable for the disaster.

The *Eastland* was raised in October, sold to the Illinois Naval Reserve, recommissioned as the USS *Wilmette*, and stationed at the Great Lakes Naval Base. The ship saw no action in either world war, and was scrapped in 1947.

30

Sverdlovsk Anthrax Leak

1979

USSR/Russia

"We are still deceiving you, Mr. Bush. We promised to eliminate bacteriological weapons. But some of our experts did everything possible to prevent me from learning the truth. It was not easy, but I outfoxed them. I caught them red-handed. I found two test sites. They are inoculating tracts of land with anthrax, allowing wild animals to go there and observing them..." —Boris Yeltsin

About 80 miles (129 km) north of Kyshtym, Russia, the scene of the 1957 nuclear disaster (see Chapter 28), is the city of Yekaterinburg (Ekaterinburg), the fourth largest city in Russia. From 1924 to 1991, during the Soviet Union era, the city was closed to outsiders and named Sverdlovsk. The city was one of the first industrial cities in Russia, because its location in the south Ural Mountains made it a crossroads between Europe and Asia.

Following World War II, Sverdlovsk became a major production center for the Soviet military-industrial complex, producing armaments, including tanks and nuclear rockets. Using captured documents from Manchuria with information about the Japanese germ warfare program, a biological weapons facility was built in Sverdlovsk.

Military Compound 19 near the city produced the most powerful strain of anthrax the Soviets had in their arsenal: Anthrax 836. The strain had been isolated when an anthrax leak occurred in Kirov in 1953. In that city, a leak from a laboratory contaminated the city's sewer system. In 1956, a more virulent strain was found in rodents captured in Kirov. This new strain would be added to warheads on SS-18 ICBMs targeting American cities.

To produce the anthrax, the culture was dried into a fine powder that could be aerosolized. The exhaust pipes in the facility in Sverdlovsk were covered with large filters, the only barriers between the anthrax dust and the air over the city.

On April 2, 1979, while the drying machines were turned off, a worker removed one of the filters so it could be unclogged. He left a note for his supervisor indicating he had done this, but the supervisor failed to enter it into the plant's logbook. The supervisor on the next shift found nothing unusual in the logbook, and resumed operation of the production line. Within a few hours, someone noticed the filter had been removed, and it was re-installed.

Within a few days, all of the workers at a ceramics factory across the street from the biological weapons lab became ill, and almost all of them were dead within a week. At least 105 died, although the exact number will never be known because the hospital records and other evidence were destroyed by the KGB, the Soviet security and intelligence agency. One of the local Communist Party bosses who helped cover up the event was Boris Yeltsin, who would become the first president of the Russian Federation from 1991 to 1999. In 1981, two years after the anthrax leak, Yeltsin was awarded the Order of Lenin for service to the Communist Party and the Soviet State.

News of the outbreak leaked to the western press in 1980, when the Russian-language German newspaper *Bild Zeitung* reported the story, claiming a thousand deaths and military occupation of the area. Over the next decade, there was considerable speculation as to whether the outbreak had been natural or accidental. If the event was an accident, the fact that the Soviets were producing anthrax would be a clear violation of the 1972 Biological Weapons Convention. The Reagan administration used intelligence about the Sverdlovsk facility, its products, and the anthrax leak to accuse the Soviet Union of violating the treaty. The Soviet government denied they had an active biological weapons program. They blamed the outbreak on handling and consumption of tainted meat. When the Soviet Union was dissolved and Soviet records became more accessible, a number of investigations of the anthrax outbreak were launched.

A senior biological weapons expert, Vladimir Pasechnik, defected to the West in 1989 and alerted Western intelligence to the scope of the Soviet bioweapons program. Pasechnik revealed that the program was 10 times the size the West had suspected. In 1992, the number two scientist in the program, Colonel Kanatjan Alibekov, defected and confirmed Pasechnik's claims. Alibekov claimed that, as of 1992, the Russians were still genetically engineering new strains of biological superweapons. President Boris Yeltsin admitted to U.S. President George H. W. Bush in 1992 that the Sverdlovsk anthrax outbreak was indeed the result of military activity at the facility. He told Bush that the KGB and military had lied to him in 1979 about the outbreak, and he promised to clean up the problem. He also claimed that the military had deceived, and was still deceiving, Yeltsin and the rest of the world, regarding the scope of ongoing biological weapons production in the former Soviet states.

Western inspectors gained access to the area, but not the plant itself, in 1992. Professor Matthew Meselson of Harvard found that all of the victims had been directly downwind of the release of the anthrax. Humans, as well as livestock, were affected in a straight line from the plant to the south. He determined that had the wind been blowing toward the city of Sverdlovsk at the time, hundreds of thousands of people would have been exposed to the spores. Meselson, who initially believed the Soviet authorities' claims that it was a natural outbreak, turned about-face and claimed the Soviets were indeed making biological weapons.

The Soviet biological weapons program dwarfed any such program in the West. In 1992, Russian Prime Minister Egor Gaidar decreed that Compound 19 would be demilitarized. Despite that, the facility continued operating, and it remains off limits to this day. Western inspectors have never been allowed to visit the facility. Classified activities have been moved underground and new laboratories have been built. It is rumored that the plant has been working with Bacillus anthracis strain H-4; its virulence and antibiotic resistance have been increased by genetic engineering. Soldiers and dogs patrol the perimeter of the complex.

Lest the reader believe that the Soviet Union was the only superpower ignoring the 1972 Biological Weapons Convention, the United States has been doing the same thing. At Dugway Proving Ground in Utah, the American military has been developing and testing chemical, biological, and radiological agents for decades. Aerial nerve agent testing took place on, and near, the installation; nearly 500,000 pounds (230,000 kg) of nerve agents were dispersed during open air tests. One of these tests of the nerve agent VX resulted in the death of more than 6,000 sheep on nearby ranches in 1968. Other weapons of mass destruction were tested in Utah, including 74 dirty bomb tests, eight tests of fallout dispersal patterns from radioactive materials, and 328 open-air tests of biological weapons. Dugway was still producing anthrax as late as 1998, although the U.S. had publicly renounced biological weapons 30 years earlier.

31

San Juanico Explosions

1984

Mexico

In the center of the town of San Juanico, Mexico, a municipal suburb 12 miles (20 km) north of Mexico City, was a massive liquid petroleum gas (LPG) tank farm. The storage and distribution facility was owned by Petroleos Mexicanos (PEMEX), the state-owned oil company. The terminal consisted of six large spherical tanks (each holding between 423,000 and 634,000 gallons (1,600 and 2,400 cubic meters) of LPG, and 48 smaller bullet-shaped tanks. On November 18, 1984, the tanks had become nearly empty, so they were filled with gas from a refinery 250 miles (400 km) away. By the next morning, November 19, the tanks contained a total of about 2,906,000 gallons (11,000 cubic meters) of a propane/butane mixture.

Operators in the control room noticed a drop in pressure at a pipeline pumping station. An 8-inch (20-cm) pipe connecting a sphere and some of the cylinders had ruptured, probably due to overfilling, but operators at the time could not identify the cause of the pressure drop. A plume of LPG, estimated to be 218 by 165 by 2 yards high (200 m by 150 m by 2 m high) formed along the ground for 10 minutes, growing enough that the wind carried it to the west side of the tank farm. The tank farm's waste gas flare pit was located there.

The plume reached the flare at 5:40 a.m. and ignited, sending a violent shock wave along the ground. The resultant vapor cloud explosion severely damaged the tank farm. LPG leaked from the damaged tanks and fed a large fire.

Only four minutes later, at 5:44 a.m., one of the tanks suffered from a boiling liquid/expanding vapor explosion (BLEVE). Within the next hour, there were 12 other separate BLEVEs. The explosions were recorded on seismographs at the University of Mexico; two of them measured 0.5 on the Richter scale. LPG rained down on the town, and surfaces covered in the liquid fuel burst into flames. The conflagration, as well as numerous explosions from the smaller tanks, continued until 10:00 a.m. the following day.

The town of San Juan Ixhuatepec surrounded the tank farm; 40,000 people lived in the town, and 60,000 more lived in the hills ringing the terminal facility, mostly in poorly-constructed small one-story houses with sheet metal roofs. The explosions blasted tank fragments as far as three-quarters of a mile (1,200 m) into the town, and destroyed many homes. Some whole cylinders weighing 30 tons (27,000 kg) went airborne. Between the explosions and the ensuing fires, much of the town was destroyed. Best estimates indicate that 500–600 people died, with 5,000–7,000 severe injuries. The intense heat from the conflagration burned practically all of the bodies beyond recognition.

Investigators later blamed a lack of safety measures in place. Issues included the layout of the plant, the lack of means to isolate an emergency situation in one part of the tank farm, the inadequacy of fire suppression systems (most of which were destroyed in the blasts), the inability of firefighters to get close to the burning tanks due to extreme heat and risk of further explosions, the lack of a gas detection system, the lack of thermal insulation on the tanks and their supports, hindrance of emergency vehicle response (traffic quickly jammed the roads as residents sought to escape the disaster), the prevalence of homes in the immediate vicinity, and the lack of a site emergency plan.

The explosions consumed all of the tank farm's 2,906,000 gallons (11,000 cubic meters) of LPG. This represented one-third of the entire LPG supply for Mexico City, one of the largest cities on the planet. It was one of the deadliest industrial disasters of all time.

32

Rana Plaza Collapse

2013

Bangladesh

"A headline that really struck me on the day of the tragedy in Bangladesh was 'Living on 38 euros a month'. That is what the people who died were being paid. This is called slave labour. Today in the world this slavery is being committed against something beautiful that God has given us — the capacity to create, to work, to have dignity. How many brothers and sisters find themselves in this situation! Not paying fairly, not giving a job because you are only looking at balance sheets, only looking at how to make a profit." —Pope Francis

The death toll in a garment factory collapse in Bangladesh in 2013 far surpassed the toll at the Sampoong Department Store (see Chapter 12). In fact, the Rana Plaza collapse was the deadliest accidental structure failure in modern human history.

The eight-story Rana Plaza, in Dhaka, Bangladesh, was home to a bank, apartments, shops, and five garment factories. Around 5,000 people worked in the building. The building's architect designed it to house shops and offices, but not factories, which require a stronger supporting structure to bear the weight of heavy, vibrating machinery. An additional four floors were added to the top of the building without a permit or inspection.

On April 23, 2013, a television crew filmed cracks in the building; when word got out, the shops and bank on the lower floors were closed and the rest of the building's occupants were evacuated. Later that day, the owner, Sohel Rana, told the media that the structure was safe and workers should return the next day. The manager of one of the factories threatened to withhold a month's pay from workers who refused to return to work.

The following morning, April 24, 2013, there was a power outage, and the huge diesel generators on the roof were started to provide electricity to the factories. During the morning rush hour, at about 8:57 a.m., the structure collapsed down to the first floor. According to the Bangladesh Garment Manufacturers and Exporters Association, 3,122 workers were in the building.

Rescue workers converged on the site and started pulling survivors from the rubble. The United Nations offered to send their International Search and Rescue Advisory Group (INSARAG) to help coordinate the recovery, but Muhiuddin Khan Alamgir, Bangladesh's Home Affairs Minister, rejected the offer, stating that no help was needed because local rescue and recovery services were well-trained and properly equipped. INSARAG re-evaluated the Bangladeshi rescue capabilities, and insisted they were not up to the task. Most of the rescue personnel responding to the disaster were volunteers and inadequately equipped. Most had no protective clothing and wore sandals. Bangladeshi officials refused outside assistance, fearing damage to the nation's pride.

Workers continued to be pulled out of the wreckage for days. When the army tried to end recovery operations, relatives of those still missing protested. On May 8, the army said that recovery of bodies would continue for another week. On May 10, seventeen days after the collapse, the last survivor was rescued, mostly unhurt from her ordeal.

Survivors reported they had to drink their own urine to survive in the scorching heat. All told, 2,515 were pulled alive from the collapsed structure. But, when the search for the dead was completed on May 13, the death toll stood at 1,129. More than half of the victims were women, and many were the workers' children who were in daycare facilities in the building.

The collapse was blamed on four shortcomings: the building was constructed without authorization, and on a pond; the building was converted from commercial to industrial use without any structural modifications to strengthen it; the building was three floors higher than it was permitted to be; and substandard building materials and practices led to structural weakness, which was aggravated by the diesel generator's vibrations.

The day after the collapse, as dozens of survivors were still being pulled out of the rubble, local officials filed cases against the building's owners and the five factories occupying the building. Sohel Rana immediately went into hiding, but he was located and arrested by security forces on April 28; four others were also arrested.

Two days after the collapse, garment workers across the capital city rioted, targeting commercial buildings and garment factories. The next day, protesters and leftist political parties demanded an independent commission to identify other dangerous factories. On May 1, which is International Workers' Day, thousands of protesters in Dhaka demanded safer working conditions, as well as the death penalty for Sohel Rana. One week later, hundreds of survivors blocked a main highway, demanding they be paid their April wages; the government assured them they would soon be paid, and the protest ended. The following day, 16 garment factories in Dhaka and two in Chittagong were closed, as the government tried to enact strict new safety measures.

On June 5, hundreds of survivors and relatives of victims protested again, demanding the pay they were promised. Police opened fire on the crowd. On June 10, seven building inspectors were accused of ignoring safety standards and renewing the licenses of the factories that had been operating in Rana Plaza.

Violent protests continued. On September 22, protesters blocked streets in Dhaka, demanding a minimum wage of $100 a month; fifty were injured when police opened fire with tear gas and rubber bullets. In November, workers burned down a 10-story garment factory in Gazipur.

The disaster quickly drew the world's attention to unsafe working conditions in factories in the developing world, especially in Bangladesh. The five factories in Rana Plaza were churning out cheap clothing for first-world retailers, such as The Children's Place, Benneton, Primark, and Walmart. According to documents pulled from the rubble, Rana Plaza garment factories were selling clothing to retailers for as low as 10% of the western retail price.

Workers were paid little more than slave's wages, with poor and dangerous working conditions. One order form showed that polo shirts were sold to retailers for USD $4.45. Those same shirts were then sold in Spain for $34–$39 and in Britain for $40–$46. Bangladeshi garment makers, paid less than half that of their counterparts in China, would have to work two to three weeks to buy one shirt. In Spain, a worker making minimum wage could buy one in a day.

Bangladesh's 4,500 garment factories employed workers as young as 11 years old. In 2013, the average wage in Bangladesh was about $64 per month, the lowest in the world; those with few skills at minimum wage earned just $38. In response to the violent protests which erupted after the Rana Plaza collapse, the minimum wage was nearly doubled.

Western retailers, trying to stay abreast of the latest rapidly changing fashions, gave short production deadlines, keeping pressure on factory owners to keep wages low and forego basic safety measures common in the developed world. Bangladeshi regulations made it difficult for labor unions to successfully fight for improved wages and conditions. State officials, of course, did not want to jeopardize the country's booming garment industry, which makes up 80% of the country's exports, by enacting regulations which would drive up clothing costs. Retrofitting factories to meet new stringent building codes would be costly, so government officials looked the other way.

In the U.S., consumers spoke out about the deplorable pay and conditions in the third-world garment industry. In July 2013, 17 major North American retailers announced plans to improve factory safety in Bangladesh; these retailers included Walmart, Target, Sears, Gap, and Macy's. However, the plan lacked legally binding commitments to pay for these improvements, and limits their liability in another disaster. Meanwhile, more than 150 other companies, mostly European, have signed the legally binding Accord on Fire and Building Safety in Bangladesh.

In March 2015, 27 protesters were arrested at the offices of The Children's Place in Secaucus, New Jersey. They were calling for the company to speed up promised compensation for victims and survivors of the Rana Plaza collapse. The protesters claimed that only $450,000 of the $30 million owed to workers' families had been paid, two years after the disaster.

By the second anniversary, 135 workers remained unaccounted for. Bulldozers long ago shoveled up the remaining debris into piles, from which human remains are still being found.

Better ways to monitor conditions and wages have been established, new labor laws have been passed, and factories are gradually being upgraded. However, most garment companies in Bangladesh continue to outsource overflow work to small, illegal, unregulated operations scattered around the country, where owners can get away with ignoring labor and safety laws. Fires in garment factories in Bangladesh continue to happen on a regular basis; it is just a matter of time before another significant garment industry disaster occurs again.

33

Los Alfaques Explosion

1978

Spain

"It was like an atomic bomb. I ran out with a fire extinguisher, but it was useless. There was nothing I could do." —Juan Derdera, employee at the Los Alfaques camp bar

Fifty-year-old Francisco Imbernón Villena pulled in to the state-owned ENPETROL refinery just north of Tarragona, Spain, at 10:15 a.m. on July 11, 1978. He was driving a semi tanker owned by Cisternas Reunidas S.A. His tanker was loaded with propylene, to be delivered to another state-owned company, Paular (now REPSOL). Workers at the refinery loaded 23 tons (20.9 metric tons) of propylene into the tanker, considerably more than the maximum load allowed, 19.35 tons (17.5 metric tons).

Imbernón's tanker left the refinery at 12:05 p.m., headed for Barcelona. Instead of taking the A-7 Motorway, Imbernón took the N-340 national road along the coast to avoid the toll on the A-7. N-340 is narrower and winds in and out of densely populated areas.

At the same time, nearly 1,000 vacationers were crowded into the Los Alfaques (The Sandbars) campsite on the side of N-340, only 1.25 miles (2 km) south of the town of Sant Carles de la Ràpita. Most of the vacationers were German, French, Belgian, and Dutch. They were packed tightly into the campground in trailers and tents.

After traveling 63 miles (102 km), Imbernón's truck reached the campsite at 2:36 p.m. It is unclear what happened at that point. There were reports that the truck was already leaking as it approached the campsite, or that there was a loud bang and the truck started leaking, and the driver pulled over to the side of the highway. Others claim that the bang was caused by a tire blowout; the truck then swerved into the wall separating the highway from the campsite, causing it to overturn.

Regardless of the direct cause, a cloud of gaseous propylene drifted into the campsite. Campers noticed the cloud and approached it out of curiosity. The cloud continued to drift toward a nearby discothèque. There, the cloud reached an ignition source, and flames flashed back to the tanker. The tanker ruptured and its contents exploded.

The ensuing blast and fireball was estimated to be at a temperature greater than 1,800°F (1,000°C). It left a crater 65 feet across and 5 feet deep (19.8 m by 1.5 m). Everything within 1,000 feet (300 m) was totally destroyed. More explosions and fires consumed what was left, as vehicle tanks and cooking gas cylinders exploded. More than 90% of the campground was gutted. The discothèque was also destroyed, killing everyone inside.

The tractor was blown almost 200 yards (170 m) from the center of the explosion. Part of the tanker flew 220 yards (200 m) through the air and landed on a nearby house. Injured campers and sunbathers on fire ran into the sea to douse the flames. The explosions killed 157 people.

For the first 45 minutes, locals attempted to evacuate survivors to hospitals. Many of them had burns covering more than 90% of their bodies. Ambulances eventually arrived. The Civil Guard and the Spanish military arrived and searched for survivors. Because the burning tanker blocked the highway, some of the injured were taken north to Amposta or Tortosa, with the most severe cases taken all the way to Barcelona. Others, on the south side of the inferno, were taken to Valencia. The last wounded survivor was removed from the scene three hours after the blast. Many of the victims taken south did not receive adequate medical attention before arriving at the hospital, and many of them died en route or after reaching the hospital.

The final death toll was 217, including the driver. More than 200 were severely burned.

During the formal inquiry which followed the disaster, Cisternas Reunidas accepted responsibility. Despite this, they denied telling drivers to avoid the tollway, saying routes are the choice of the driver. ENPETROL denied any responsibility, as cargo delivery is the responsibility of the carrier. The inquiry concluded that the tanker was severely overloaded and lacked emergency pressure release valves which are designed to prevent a boiling liquid/expanding vapor explosion (BLEVE). However, by 1978 these valves were no longer mandatory. The truck had passed all of its recent inspections.

The inquiry also uncovered the fact that the tanker, when it was constructed in 1973, did not meet requirements for carrying flammable liquids, since it did not have the release valves. Therefore, the tanker was used to carry other liquids, some of them corrosive. Tests on the remains of the tanker showed that previous loads of improperly pressurized anhydrous ammonia had created stress fractures. If the tanker had received structural damage during the initial stages of the disaster, it would explain the nearly instantaneous rupture of the tanker when the flames flashed back from the discothèque. Investigators concluded that, even without safety release valves, a properly filled tanker should be able to maintain structural integrity in a fire long enough to allow nearby people to escape.

The inquiry revealed other distressing facts. Overloading of tankers was commonplace at ENPETROL refineries. The refinery at Tarragona did not have a meter to indicate the amount of gas that had been dispensed, nor did it have an automatic shut-off system to prevent tank overfilling. Therefore, most tankers were consistently overfilled. Imbernón was not told that his tank had been overfilled, or exactly what class of flammable liquid he was transporting. There was no way for him to check the pressure level either before he left the terminal, or while en route. Cisternas Reunidas had not sent Imbernón to HAZMAT training because they considered him experienced enough, with 20 years of experience driving tankers.

In response to the disaster, Spanish authorities prohibited the transport of dangerous cargo through populated areas. Four ENPETROL employees and two Cisternas Reunidas employees were convicted in 1982 of criminal negligence and sentenced to prison for one to four years. After a legal appeal, four were released, and prison sentences were reduced or suspended. The two companies paid a total of €13.23 million in compensation to the victims.

Six months after the explosion, the Los Alfaques campsite had been renovated and was open to tourists again. Later, the owners sued Google through the Spanish courts. The owners were dismayed that, decades after the disaster, the top 12 results of a Google search of "Los Alfaques camping" brings up information on the disaster as well as disturbing images of human remains, which negatively affects their business. The plaintiffs sued under provisions of the European Union's 2012 "Right to Be Forgotten" Act, seeking to free themselves from the stigma of a past event. The trial was dismissed; the court ruled that the plaintiffs would have to pursue the case in U.S. Courts since Google is an American company. No such law has yet been adopted in the U.S.

34

Sinking of the *Wilhelm Gustloff*

1945

Baltic Sea

"We all felt we had no more hope. We could not cry for help anymore, our horrified cry is still in my ears, and I will never forget it as long as I live. We had just given up, drifting in the cold water. There was a little boy in the boat, 8 or 9 years old. He kept on saying, "Let's yell one more time, then we will be saved, don't give up." With our last effort in chorus, we cried out "Help, help, help!" I still hear that cry. . . We all knew we could not last much longer." —Rose Petrus, survivor

The MV *Wilhelm Gustloff* was built as a cruise ship for the Nazi organization Kraft durch Freude (Strength Through Joy) in 1937. The original intention was to name the ship the *Adolph Hitler*, but Hitler changed his mind and named it after Wilhelm Gustloff, a leader of the Swiss Branch of the National Socialist Party. He had been assassinated in 1936.

When war broke out in Europe in 1939, the *Wilhelm Gustloff* was requisitioned by the Kriegsmarine, the German Navy, to serve as a hospital ship in 1939 and 1940, then as a floating barracks for U-boat trainees in the port of Gdynia (in present-day Poland). In 1945, as the German Reich collapsed, she was put into service to help transport refugees.

The evacuation of German troops and civilians from Courland, East Prussia, and Danzig-West Prussia was code named "Operation Hannibal." Stories about Soviet revenge for the Nazi invasion of the Soviet Union panicked civilians, who needed safe passage west to Germany. As the Red Army advanced on German positions, military personnel, technicians, and refugees needed transport from the advanced weapons bases in the Baltic Sea to Kiel.

The *Wilhelm Gustloff* left Gdynia (called Gotenhafen by the Germans) on January 30, 1945, packed with refugees; thousands more were left behind at the harbor for lack of room. She was accompanied by the *Hansa*, a passenger liner also loaded with civilians and military personnel, and two torpedo boats. The *Wilhelm Gustloff*'s passenger manifest indicates there were 6,050 people on board, but many civilians boarded without being recorded. A *Wilhelm Gustloff* survivor, Heinz Schön, later determined that she was carrying 918 officers and U-boat trainees, a crew of 173 navy armed forces auxiliaries, 373 female naval auxiliary members, 162 wounded soldiers, and 8,956 civilians, 5,000 of them children, for a grand total of 10,582 souls on board.

Soon after leaving port, the *Hansa* and one of the torpedo boats developed mechanical problems and had to return to port. Friedrich Petersen, the *Wilhelm Gustloff*'s captain, ignored the advice of the military commander, who wanted the ship to travel close to shore in shallow water and without lights to avoid submarine attacks. Instead, the *Wilhelm Gustloff* headed for deeper water which had been cleared of mines.

The ship received a mysterious radio message saying there was an oncoming German minesweeper convoy, so the captain activated the ship's navigation lights to avoid a collision. The source of this radio message, and its authenticity, were never confirmed, and no convoy was present.

The *Wilhelm Gustloff* had been outfitted with anti-aircraft guns, and because she was transporting military personnel, the ship did not qualify under the rules of war as a hospital ship. The Germans felt compelled to obey these rules, and hence she was not marked as a hospital ship.

With her lights ablaze, the *Wilhelm Gustloff* was quickly seen by a Soviet submarine, *S-13*, under the command of Captain Alexander Marinesko. He followed the ship for two hours. The submarine sensor on the torpedo boat was inoperable, as were the anti-aircraft guns on the *Wilhelm Gustloff*; both had become coated in ice and were immobilized. The *S-13* fired three torpedoes at about 9:00 p.m. on January 30, 1945 as the ships passed about 19 miles (30 km) offshore near Łeba, Poland in the Baltic Sea.

The first torpedo, on which had been written "For the Motherland," struck the port bow. The second, labeled "For the Soviet People," hit amidships. The third torpedo, "For Leningrad," struck the engine room beneath the ship's funnel. A fourth torpedo, "For Stalin," misfired and was disarmed before it could blow the submarine to pieces.

The first torpedo caused the watertight doors to seal off the bow, where all the off-duty crew members were sleeping. The second torpedo hit the accommodations for the women's naval auxiliary; 370 of the 373 women there were killed outright when the blast sent fragments of decorative mosaic tiles sailing through the room's occupants. The third torpedo hit the engine room directly, cutting off all power and communications. Only one lifeboat was lowered before the *Wilhelm Gustloff* sank.

Typically, at that time of year, the water temperature in the Baltic would be about 39°F (4°C). On this night, the air temperature was between 0 and 14°F (-18 to -10°C). Ice floes covered the surface. Those who hadn't been killed in the torpedo explosions either drowned in the onrushing water, were crushed in the panic, or perished when they jumped into the icy water.

In only 40 minutes, the *Wilhelm Gustloff* was lying on her side in 144 feet (44 m) of water. Thousands of people were trapped inside the ship.

German forces arrived quickly and rescued 1,252 survivors.

Using Heinz Schön's calculations, that left 9,343 dead in the sinking, about 5,000 of them children. It was the largest loss of life from the sinking of a single vessel in history. More recent research for the Discovery Channel's program *Unsolved History* in 2003 confirms that approximately 9,400 of the 10,600 people aboard died. The vessel was designed with a maximum capacity of 1,880 passengers and crew.

An official naval inquiry was started against Lieutenant Commander Wilhelm Zahn, the military commander of the ship. The case was never resolved as the Nazi government collapsed shortly thereafter.

Many ships carrying civilians were sunk by both sides in World War II. Just 11 days after the *Wilhelm Gustloff* sinking, the *S-13* sank the *General von Steuben* and 3,000 more people lost their lives. After that sinking, Hitler declared Alexander Marinesko a "personal enemy." On April 16, 1945, while also taking part in Operation Hannibal, MV *Goya* was sunk by a Soviet submarine; there were 183 survivors out of about 6,700 passengers and crew. The SS *Cap Arcona* was filled with prisoners from Nazi concentration camps when she was sunk by the British Royal Air Force, killing about 5,000, with another 2,750 dead in sunken vessels accompanying her (the *Thielbek* and the SS *Deutschland*). The MV *Awa Maru*, a Japanese ocean liner, was torpedoed by an American submarine, the USS *Queenfish*, who mistook the Red Cross relief ship as a destroyer; only one of the 2,004 people on the ship survived. (Incidentally, it was the third time that Kantora Shimoda had been the sole survivor of a torpedoed ship.) The British liner RMS *Lancastria* was sunk by a Nazi air assault on June 17, 1940, with a loss of at least 4,000 people, in the highest death toll of any British engagement in the war. The Soviet hospital ship *Armenia* was struck by German aircraft on November 7, 1941; between 5,000 and 7,000 people were killed. All told, during World War II, 50 ship sinkings due to submarine attacks had death tolls of more than 1,000 on each ship. Many others were sunk by aerial bombardment.

Despite the massive loss of life, Operation Hannibal was successful in bringing 2,000,000 Germans to safety in the West.

The *Wilhelm Gustloff* is one of the largest shipwrecks on the floor of the Baltic. To protect the site, Poland has forbidden diving within 1,600 feet (500 m) of the wreck.

35

Yellow River Flood and Changsha Fire

1938

China

Prior to 1937, the Empire of Japan had sought for decades to expand its military and political influence in Asia. Japan wished to secure its access to raw materials, food, and human labor. Eventually, in 1937, war broke out as Japan invaded and attempted to occupy portions of mainland Asia, including the Korean Peninsula, Formosa (now Taiwan), and Manchuria in China. This war was called the Second Sino-Japanese War.

After Japan attacked Pearl Harbor in 1941, the U.S. and U.S.S.R. provided financial support to the Chinese to repel the Japanese invaders, and the war merged into the Pacific Theater of War as part of World War II.

After the war began in 1937, the Imperial Japanese Army quickly occupied a significant portion of China, including the capital city of Nanking. By June 1938, all of North China was under Japanese control and the major cities of Wuhan and Xi'an were threatened.

In a desperate move to prevent the Japanese from advancing any further, Chiang Kai-shek, the Chinese leader, decided to open the dikes along the Huang He (Yellow River) near Zhengzhou. The dikes were destroyed at Huayuankou on June 5 and June 7. Water poured into the provinces of Henan, Anhui, and Jiangsu. In a modified scorched-earth tactic, thousands of square kilometers of farmland were destroyed. Thousands of villages were flooded and destroyed, leaving several million Chinese as homeless refugees. The mouth of the Yellow River shifted several hundred miles south.

A post-war commission determined that 800,000 people drowned, although the true number will never be known. With China in a state of war, much of the general population and government officials had fled the area, so there was no count of the dead. After the war, the government claimed 12 million people had been affected by the flood, with 800,000 deaths. An official government history of the war published in 1994 claimed 900,000 deaths and 10 million refugees. Recent studies have concluded the death toll was more likely 400,000–500,000, with three million refugees and 5,000,000 people affected.

The Nationalist Chinese government initially claimed the dike breach was the result of Japanese bombings, and showed the great sacrifice the Chinese people had made.

Strategically, the flood did little to stop the Japanese invaders. Few Japanese troops were in the area at the time, and most of the important towns and transportation lines in the flooded area had already been captured. The city of Wuhan was eventually attacked from a different direction and taken. However, the Japanese were ultimately unable to consolidate their control over the flooded area.

It took years for the area to recover. The crops were destroyed and covered in silt, making the countryside uncultivable for years. Much of the infrastructure and many of the buildings were destroyed.

The Chinese people, who eventually learned the truth about the dike breach, blamed both the Japanese invaders and the Chinese government for the disaster. Their anger toward their own government led to Chinese Communists using the flooded area as recruiting grounds. By the 1940s, a large guerrilla base was located in the area. The Communists attempted to prevent the Chinese government, with the help of the United Nations, from rebuilding the dikes because it was a successful rallying point. Although the dikes were rebuilt in 1946 and 1947, the Communists had received a huge boost in northern China.

The "Huayuankou Embankment Breach Event," as the disaster is referred to in China, is considered the largest act of environmental warfare in history.

The Yellow River Flood was not the last attempt at a scorched-earth strategy by the Chinese during the Second Sino-Japanese War. When Wuhan fell in October 1938, refugees poured into Changsha. Soon, Japanese forces had advanced to the Xinqiang River just outside of Changsha. Believing the Chinese could not hold the city, Chiang Kai-shek suggested burning Changsha to the ground so there would be nothing left for the Japanese if they entered the city. Fires were lit early November 13, 1938; the city burned for five days. Over 90% of the city's structures burned. The death toll was over 30,000.

The tactic turned out to be unnecessary. Three Japanese attacks in 1939, 1941, and 1942 were repulsed. Changsha finally fell to the Japanese in 1944, but by that point the city was no longer strategically important.

36

Hyatt Regency Hotel Walkway Collapse
1981

Missouri, USA

"We don't know what we can accomplish, what we can withstand, until we are tested. The will to live is pretty strong." —Deputy Fire Chief Arnett Williams, incident commander

On the evening of July 17, 1981, nearly 1,600 people gathered in the atrium of the Hyatt Regency Hotel in Kansas City, Missouri for a tea dance. The 40-story hotel was only a year old. The lobby was a multistory atrium, measuring 117 feet (36 m) by 145 feet (44 m) and 50 feet (15 m) high; elevated walkways made of glass, steel, and concrete were suspended from the ceiling and connected the north and south wings on the second, third, and fourth floors. Each of the three bridges weighed about 64,000 pounds (29,000 kg) and was 120 feet (37 m) long.

Most of the people at the dance were on the main floor, but about 40 people were on the second-floor walkway, and 16 to 20 were on the fourth-floor walkway, watching the celebration below. At 7:05 p.m., the fourth-floor walkway suddenly collapsed, and fell onto the second-floor walkway, which was directly below it. Both walkways then fell onto the crowd below. The third-floor walkway was undamaged, as it was offset from the other two.

Rescue crews rushed to the scene. Thirty-four fire crews and EMS units arrived, as did doctors from five local hospitals. Local hospitals were warned to expect victims from a mass-casualty event. Employees of a construction company resurfacing a parking garage across the street arrived with hydraulic jacks, torches, and generators to help remove debris to reach victims trapped under the rubble. Kansas City's disaster response team arrived with earthmoving equipment, and cranes arrived to lift sections of steel and concrete.

Medical responders set up a triage area in front of the hotel, and set up a morgue in the hotel's exhibition area. The walking wounded were put on city buses and taken to hospitals. More seriously injured victims were airlifted by helicopter to the city's hospitals.

Rescuers found themselves with no choice but to dismember bodies in order to reach and free survivors trapped under the wreckage. In one case, an injured survivor, with a leg trapped under an I-beam, had to have his right leg amputated by a surgeon with a chainsaw; the victim later died.

The falling wreckage severed the hotel's sprinkler system. The lobby slowly filled with water, putting trapped survivors at risk for drowning. The flow could not be stopped because the pipes were not connected to a public water source, but instead were connected to water tanks without shut-off valves. The last survivor pulled from the rubble alive had spent more than nine-and-a-half hours trapped under the lower skywalk and nearly drowned. Upon freeing the survivor, the fire chief realized the water was rising in the lobby, and he had a bulldozer smash the front windows to release the pooling water. The fire department then placed a fire hose over the broken pipe and diverted the water flow outside.

During the rescue operation, the power had been cut to prevent a fire from breaking out. Visibility was poor for rescuers because of the low lighting, and concrete dust in the air from the collapse and the cutting and removal of debris.

By 2:00 a.m., hundreds of concerned Kansas City residents had lined up to donate blood at the local blood center.

In the end, 29 people were pulled alive from the rubble, and 111 bodies were recovered. Three more people died after being taken to local hospitals. The injured numbered 216. The rescue operation lasted 14 hours. The disaster was the deadliest structural collapse in American history until the south tower of the World Trade Center fell during the terrorist attacks of September 11, 2001.

The *Kansas City Star* hired an architectural engineer to determine the cause of the collapse. Within three days of the disaster, the engineer discovered a change in the original design of the walkways. Both walkways were suspended from a set of steel tie rods 1.25 inch (32 mm) across. The fourth-floor walkway was supported by three cross beams suspended by steel rods, held in place by nuts. The cross beams were made from C-channel strips welded together lengthwise, with hollow space along the length. It was later determined that this design could support only 60% of the minimum load required by the building codes in Kansas City.

The contractor responsible for manufacturing the rods objected to the original design because it required the entire rod to be screw threaded from the second-floor walkway all the way to the fourth floor in order to thread the nut that would hold the fourth-floor walkway in place. They believed the threads would be damaged as the walkways were lifted into position during construction. They proposed a change in the design; instead of long vertical rods supporting both walkways, separate rods supporting the second-floor walkway would be hung offset from the fourth-floor rods, suspending the lower walkway from the upper one.

This design change meant that the fourth-floor support structure was supporting both walkways, so this design could only bear 30% of the weight loaded onto it.

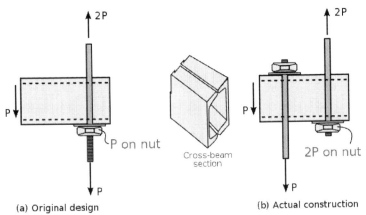

(a) Original design   (b) Actual construction

The design flaw was made worse by the fact that the bolts were put through the two C-channels directly where they were welded together, the weakest spot on the beams. Examination of the wreckage revealed that these channels split and peeled away along the welded seam, letting the support rods slip completely through the deformed support beam as the structure collapsed.

Investigators came to the conclusion that the design company and contractor had not performed basic calculations that would have revealed the design flaw. Each group believed the other had done the necessary calculations to verify the structural integrity of the design. In an era of high unemployment, inflation, and interest rates, builders in the 1970s and early 1980s were pressured to win contracts and complete building projects as quickly as they could.

In response to these revelations, the engineers responsible were charged with negligence, misconduct, and unprofessional conduct and had their engineering licenses revoked. The engineering firm responsible lost its license.

Subsequent lawsuits led to judgments and settlements being awarded to victims and their families for at least $140 million, mostly paid by Crown Center Corporation, the owner of the property.

Several rescuers suffered from mental health problems after the disaster, and one jackhammer operator later took his own life.

The walkway collapse was not the first problem at the hotel. During construction, on October 14, 1979, 27,000 square feet (250 square meters) of the atrium roof collapsed. This collapse was blamed on the failure of one of the roof connections. The main engineering firm promised to check all structural connections in the building as construction resumed.

After the disaster, the lobby was rebuilt with only one walkway overhead, on the second floor. It was supported by columns underneath instead of a support structure that hung from the ceiling. The hotel reopened three months after the disaster. Subsequent hotel renovations have kept the same atrium design. The hotel was renamed the Sheraton Kansas City at Crown Center in 2011.

The disaster is still a classic model for studying engineering errors and ethics, as well as disaster management. Each principal in the engineering of the Hyatt's walkways pointed the finger at others and denied responsibility, so stricter guidelines defining professional responsibilities for engineers, as well as consequences for failing to uphold those responsibilities, were put in place. In Kansas City, changes were made so a single city engineer would review all building plans for construction projects before the city would approve the plan, to make sure the pieces of the plan fit together properly. Previously, multiple engineers would be involved, each reviewing a specific part of the whole, with no one overseeing the entire project.

On July 17, 2015 ground was broken in a park across the street from the hotel for a permanent memorial to the victims, survivors, and first responders of the walkway collapse, as well as their families.

37

Kursha-2 Firestorm

1936

USSR/Russia

Kursha-2 was a town built southeast of Moscow after the October Revolution of 1917. A small industrial community, Kursha-2's purpose was to harvest wood from the local forests and transport it to Tumskaya via a narrow-gauge railway. The population was over 1,000 in the 1930s.

On August 1, 1936, a firestorm erupted near Charus, south of Kursha-2. A firestorm can be man-made or a natural phenomenon; the fire can become so intense it creates and sustains its own storm-force winds from all directions. Australia's Black Saturday Bushfires of 2009 and Wisconsin's Peshtigo Fire of 1871 (see Chapter 46) are examples of firestorms which have caused a large loss of life. The firebombings of Tokyo, Hamburg, and Dresden, as well as the atomic bombing of Hiroshima, also led to firestorms.

As the original fire quickly spreads and builds intensity, a strong updraft develops and draws fresh air from all directions into the center of the fire. The strong turbulence continues to cause strong gale-forced inflow winds, and the conflagration becomes even more intense. A particularly strong firestorm may also develop into a mesocyclone and create fire whirls, actual tornadoes made of fire. A fire whirl is also known as a fire tornado or firenado. The intense heat of a firestorm can ignite flammable material ahead of the actual fire; this also expands the intensity of the fire, as well as the area it covers. The inflow also sucks combustible material into the storm itself, also increasing the storm's intensity, to the point where extremely high temperatures melt asphalt, metal, and glass. Eventually the firestorm consumes everything that is combustible within reach, so the turbulent winds decrease until the fire burns itself out.

The Charus firestorm quickly spread north, threatening Kursha-2. On the night of August 2, 1936, an empty train made it to Kursha-2 to evacuate women and children from the logging town. However, the local dispatcher ordered a load of wood to also be loaded onto the train. The resultant delay prevented the train's departure until the firestorm reached the town the next day.

There was not enough room on the train for everyone who wanted to escape the town. Hundreds were left behind at the station. Refugees rode away on the engine, the wood logs, and even on the couplings between the rail cars.

North of Kursha-2, the train, overloaded with woodcutters and their families, railway workers, and military personnel, reached a bridge over a canal that was burning. The train caught fire and burned on the bridge.

Twenty people escaped by jumping into the water or by seeking refuge on a deforested hill, but about 1,200 people died.

The town was rebuilt to some degree, but, following World War II, when the resources around Kursha-2 were depleted, the railway was dismantled and the town abandoned. Today, all that remains is a few old ruins and a cross that marks the mass grave of victims.

A cross marking the mass grave where Kursha-2 firestorm victims were buried is about all that remains of the town.

38

Le Joola Ferry Capsizing

2002

Gambia

"A father who loses all his children, all of them... it has been very difficult. Every day they come back into my head because my whole universe was built around them. They were my life. I feel traumatized whenever their birthdays are here because I wish I could celebrate with them, make them happy, and watch them celebrating. But no... they are gone because of the recklessness and negligence of some government officials." —Idrissa Diallo, whose three children died on the *Le Joola*

MV *Le Joola* was a roll-on/roll-off ferry built in Germany and put to sea in 1990. She was 259 feet (79 m) long and was equipped with the latest safety equipment. The *Le Joola* carried 44 crew, and could carry 35 automobiles and 536 passengers. It was owned by the Senegalese government and traveled between Ziguinchor and Dakar, the capital of Senegal, along the Atlantic coast of West Africa twice a week. The route was popular because landmines and attacks by separatist rebels had made the overland route dangerous. Many of its passengers were women who sold mangoes and palm oil at the Dakar market.

Ziguinchor is in southern Senegal and Dakar is farther north along the coast. The ferry's route took it off the shore of the country of The Gambia, which is surrounded by Senegal. On September 26, 2002, the *Le Joola* set sail at about 1:30 p.m., headed for Dakar. Despite the official capacity of crew and passengers of 580, the ferry was carrying about 1,927 people. The exact number will never be known; 1,034 passengers held tickets, but the rest of the passengers were either not required to have a ticket because they were less than five years old, or they were granted free passage and therefore were not required to hold a ticket. (In many third world countries, the tradition is to allow destitute people to travel for free.) At the island of Carabane, 185 people had boarded despite the absence of a formal port of entry.

At 10:00 p.m., the *Le Joola* radioed the maritime security center in Dakar that travel conditions were good. The ship was designed to be used in coastal waters, and its operational license restricted it to the coast, but the ship regularly traveled a more direct line to Dakar, taking it out into the open Atlantic. In open seas more than 12 miles (20 km) off the coast of Gambia, at about 11:00 p.m., the *Le Joola* sailed into a storm. The rough seas and the wind caused the ship to list; unsecured cargo slid across the decks and the ship capsized, dumping passengers and cargo into the sea.

Many of the passengers drowned when the ship capsized; a large number survived but drowned while waiting to be rescued. Others were trapped alive inside the overturned ferry.

During the night, local fishermen started pulling a few survivors and some of the dead bodies out of the Atlantic. Official rescue teams did not arrive until the next morning; radio operators had been absent from their posts overnight and were not aware of the capsizing. At 2:00 p.m., a 15-year-old boy was rescued; he confirmed that many people were still trapped alive inside the *Le Joola*, and rescuers could hear screaming from within.

The *Le Joola* stayed afloat until 3:00 p.m., when she finally sank 59 feet (18 m) to the bottom of the ocean, drowning the remaining trapped passengers. Only 64 people had been rescued alive, including only one woman. The death toll has been estimated to be 1,863.

Two days later, a diving team led by environmental activist Haïdar El Ali explored the wreck. They found no survivors, but did find many bodies of men, women, and children trapped inside the ship. The team recovered 551 dead bodies. Only 93 were identifiable and were turned over to relatives; the rest were interred in specially-built cemeteries in Kabadiou, Kantene, Mbao, and along the

Gambian coast. More than half of the victims were never recovered.

El Ali's team had the equipment to raise the wreck and retrieve the rest of the bodies, but the government was silent on whether it should or shouldn't be raised.

The massive death toll stunned the Senegalese, and the government quickly convened an inquiry. The accident was caused by a number of factors. The ship was sailing beyond coastal waters, to which it was restricted, with wind and waves the direct cause of the capsizing. The ship held about three times as many people as it was designed to carry; most of the additional passengers were sleeping on the top decks, making the ferry more unstable and prone to capsizing. The *Le Joola* was only 12 years old, but had a history of maintenance problems in the previous year; indeed, the ship had been out of service for most of the previous year for repairs. It was relaunched on September 10, possibly under pressure because the Gambian government had raised the fee to cross the Gambia River to reach northern Senegal. Poorly-paid ferry officials were also accused of taking bribes to allow extra passengers on board. The official government report also blamed poor training of the crew, the failure of the captain to calculate the ship's stability before leaving port, and inadequate emergency rafts.

In response to the disaster, the Senegalese government fired several officials and offered reparations of US$22,000 per victim. Some high-ranking officials within the Armed Forces of Senegal were charged with failure to respond quickly to the disaster and moved to other posts. However, no individuals were ever blamed for allowing the *Le Joola* to sail outside coastal waters or with so many more passengers than it was allowed to carry. No one was ever charged or prosecuted for the deaths.

There were, however, political repercussions. On September 26, President Abdoulaye Wade announced that the government was accepting full responsibility for the disaster. The Transport Minister and the Armed Forces Minister resigned. Prime Minister Mame Madior Boye and much of her cabinet were dismissed by President Wade for mishandling the rescue. During the 2007 presidential election, President Wade's rival accused him of covering up government responsibility for the disaster. Families of the dead continue to criticize the Senegalese government for the slow response time, the ferry operation, and the difficulty in receiving reparations.

In 2005, the European Union provided a grant to Senegal to raise the wreck, but the Senegalese government would not allow that to happen.

A new German ferry was pressed into service on the Ziguinchor-to-Dakar route. Passenger capacity is now strictly enforced.

The capsizing of the *Le Joola* is the second-worst non-military maritime disaster in history. The worst is the sinking of the MV *Doña Paz* in 1987 (see chapter 42); the sinking of the RMS *Titanic* ranks as the third worst.

39

Texas City Explosions

1947

Texas, USA

"Here comes another explosion — you have just heard it. The sky is like broad daylight." —Ben Kaplan, KTHT news in Houston, broadcasting live coverage of the second explosion over the radio

The SS *Grandcamp*, a French-registered vessel, was docked in the port city of Texas City, Texas, on April 16, 1947. In its cargo hold were about 2,300 tons (2,100 metric tons) of ammonium nitrate, small arms ammunition, peanuts, and machinery, with bales of sisal twine loaded on its deck. Docked about 600 feet (200 m) away was the SS *High Flyer*, with 961 tons (872 metric tons) of ammonium nitrate and 1,800 tons (1,600 metric tons) of sulfur. The ammonium nitrate in both ships and in a nearby warehouse was being shipped to farmers in Europe as part of post-war reconstruction.

Ammonium nitrate is used as a fertilizer as well as an explosive. It is the same explosive which was used to destroy the Oklahoma City federal building in 1995. The ammonium nitrate in the *Grandcamp* and *High Flyer* had been manufactured in Nebraska and Iowa and was shipped to Texas City by rail. When it was manufactured, it was mixed with clay, petrolatum, rosin, and paraffin wax to prevent moisture caking. It was then packaged in paper sacks and transported and stored at temperatures that encouraged chemical activity within the package. When the sacks were loaded onto the ships, longshoremen reported the bags were warm to the touch.

About 8:00 that morning, while the *Grandcamp* was still docked, smoke was spotted in the cargo hold. The ship's crew attempted to put the fire out, but was unsuccessful. Shortly before 9:00 a.m., the captain ordered firefighters to steam the hold; steam would be piped in to douse the fire and preserve the cargo. This, however, proved to be ineffective, since ammonium nitrate produces oxygen, which would actually feed a fire, and steam added to the cargo of ammonium nitrate would convert it to nitrous oxide, augmenting the heat of the ongoing chemical reaction.

A crowd of people lined the shore, watching the firefighting operation, as was common when fires broke out in the port. Soon, the ship's hatches blew open because of the steam pressure in the hold; yellow-orange smoke billowed from the ship. Even more spectators were attracted to the shore because of the color of the smoke. Spectators believed they were far enough away from the action and were not in danger.

The crowd noticed that the seawater around the ship was boiling due to the intense heat from the fire. Water splashing against the hull was being vaporized into steam. The cargo hold and decks were bulging because of the intense steam pressure inside the ship.

The captain gave the abandon ship order, but most of the crew remained nearby.

At 9:12 a.m., the ammonium nitrate reached its explosive threshold of 850°F (454°C) and detonated in a massive blast. The explosion, one of the largest non-nuclear explosions in history, leveled almost 1,000 buildings. It destroyed the Monsanto Chemical Company plant and ignited refineries and chemical tanks lining the harbor. Fires raged everywhere in the town.

The explosion hurled 6,350 tons (5,760 metric tons) of steel from the *Grandcamp* into the sky, some of it at supersonic speeds, as high as 2,000 to 3,000 feet (600 to 900 m). Bales of burning twine from the *Grandcamp*'s deck fell from the sky, as did two sightseeing airplanes flying nearby when their wings were torn off. The *Grandcamp*'s 2-ton (1.8-metric ton) anchor was thrown 1.62 miles (2.61 km) across the city, and can still be seen in a memorial park. Another 5-ton (4.5-metric ton) anchor was thrown one-half mile (0.8 km); it, too, is still there, part of another memorial.

In Galveston, 10 miles (16 km) away, the blast forced people to their knees. An oily fog soon settled over the city, covering all surfaces. Windows were broken in Baytown, 25 miles (40 km) away, and in Houston, 40 miles (64 km) away. The shockwave was even felt in Louisiana, 250 miles (400 km) away. The blast sent a 15-foot (4.5 m) tsunami out to sea; the wave was measurable nearly 100 miles (160 km) off the coast in the Gulf of Mexico. This wave carried ships in the port inland about 200 feet (61 m) and swept through the remains of the Monsanto Chemical Company's plant. The explosion registered on a seismograph in Denver, Colorado.

Numerous witnesses reported a second blast within five seconds, and then a third blast.

The official death toll from the explosion was 567. All of the crew members remaining on the *Grandcamp* died. All but one member of the 29-man Texas City Fire Department were killed; they were on the dock attempting to douse the flames in the *Grandcamp*'s hold. All four city fire engines were destroyed. The lone firefighting survivor, who hadn't responded to the fire, helped coordinate firefighters who soon started arriving from other communities as far away as

Los Angeles.

The explosion ignited the ammonium nitrate in the *High Flyer*, which had been docked nearby. The blast had torn the *High Flyer* loose from its moorings and it was now entangled in moorings against the SS *Wilson B. Keene*. Crews attempted to cut the ship free of her anchor, but were not successful. Ten hours after the *Grandcamp* blast, smoke started pouring out of the *High Flyer's* hold, and five hours after that, at 1:12 a.m. on April 17, the *High Flyer* blew up. The SS *Wilson B. Keene* was destroyed too, and shrapnel and fire inflicted more damage on the port and the city. Warehouse (Pier) A completely collapsed. At least two more people died there. One of the *High Flyer's* propellers was blown a mile (1.6 km) inland. Casualties were limited because detonation seemed inevitable once the *High Flyer* caught fire; in fact, the explosion was broadcast live over a Houston radio station.

The Texas City explosions are considered the deadliest industrial accident in American history. Witnesses compared the devastation to that of Nagasaki from two years earlier. The central business district of Texas City suffered serious damage; two theaters had their roofs collapse, and city hall was damaged severely. Most windows in the city facing the port were blown out, as were many doors and roofs.

Authorities were able to identify 405 of the dead; 63 were never identified. Another 113 were classified as missing; no identifiable parts of them were ever found. This included the firefighters aboard the *Grandcamp*.

Surprisingly, there were survivors of the blast as close as 70 feet (21 m) to the dock. Many of those who survived had blood streaming out of their noses and ears from the blast concussion.

The count of the injured topped 5,000, and 1,784 were admitted to 21 hospitals in the area. Many children were injured by flying glass and collapsing walls and ceilings at schools over a mile (1.6 km) away. More than 500 homes were destroyed, and hundreds more damaged, leaving 2,000 residents homeless. More than 1,100 vehicles and 362 rail cars and their contents were damaged or destroyed. The seaport was destroyed. Property damage was estimated at $100,000,000 (more than $1 billion today).

A week later, fires still burned out of control around the port. It took nearly a month to recover all the bodies.

Hundreds of lawsuits were filed; many were combined into *Elizabeth Dalehite, et al. v. United States*, the first class-action lawsuit against the U.S. government. The lawsuits were brought under the newly-enacted Federal Tort Claims Act (FTCA) on behalf of 8,485 victims. Some 168 agencies and their representatives were accused of being responsible for the manufacture, packaging, transport, and handling of the fertilizer, as well as for fire prevention and suppression. The case eventually made it to the Supreme Court, but the plaintiffs did not prevail, as the courts ruled that the FTCA exempts "failure to exercise or perform a discretionary function or duty," and, according to the courts, all of the alleged acts were discretionary. Because the courts refused to provide compensation, Congress stepped in and granted financial relief. By 1957, 1,394 awards for a total nearing $17 million had been made.

There is evidence that the fire on the *Grandcamp* was possibly started by a cigarette discarded the day before the blast. As the cargo hatch was battened down, a fire could have smoldered for a day before being discovered.

The final report by the Fire Prevention and Engineering Bureau of Texas blamed the disaster in part on improper package labeling (nothing on the packaging indicated it was a hazardous material) and improper storage standards for ammonium nitrate. The report also recommended that smoking be prohibited on shipping docks and while hazardous cargo is being handled, that all ports and industrial centers have disaster plans in place, and that manifests of the cargoes of ships carrying hazardous materials be submitted to local fire departments upon arrival in port.

Because of the necessity of coordination between various disaster response agencies, the Texas City explosions did indeed trigger widespread disaster response plans to be enacted at the local and regional level.

But the Texas City disaster would not be the last time people died from an accidental detonation of ammonium nitrate. In 1959, a discarded cigarette started a fire which detonated two tons (1.8 metric tons) of dynamite and one-half ton (0.45 metric tons) of ammonium nitrate on a truck in downtown Roseburg, Oregon. Eight city blocks were leveled, a 52-foot (16-m) crater 12 feet (3.6 m) deep was made, and 14 people died. The only reason the death toll wasn't substantially higher was that the blast occurred at 2:00 a.m.

An ammonium nitrate plant caught fire in West, Texas, on April 17, 2013. While the local fire department attempted to douse the flames, the plant blew up, killing 15 (10 of them first responders), injuring 160, and destroying or damaging 150 buildings. The blast registered as a 2.1-magnitude earthquake.

On August 12, 2015, a series of blasts in a container storage area in the port of Tianjin, China, left 159 dead, 14 missing, and 797 injured. The initial blast originated with hazardous materials being stored at the facility. Secondary blasts continued for four days. The first blast measured as a magnitude 2.3 earthquake; the second explosion, the largest, was photographed by an orbiting Japanese satellite.

Disaster would strike the port of Texas City again. On March 23, 2005, a hydrocarbon vapor cloud exploded at a BP refinery in Texas City, resulting in 15 deaths and 170 injuries.

Courtesy of Special Collections, University of Houston Libraries.
A parking lot a quarter-mile from the blast.

Courtesy of Special Collections, University of Houston Libraries.
The nearby Monsanto Chemical Company plant, completely
destroyed.

40

Zolitude Shopping Center Collapse

2013

Latvia

"We now have 54 fallen victims at Zolitūde, not from bullets, but rather from the blank spots in our national legislation." —Arturs Kaimiņš, politician in the Latvian opposition party, comparing the victims to veteran soldiers fallen on the battlefield

The Zolitūde shopping center in Riga, the capital of Latvia, opened in November 2011. The building was awarded a national architectural prize when it was completed. It was home to a bank, currency exchange, a pet store, a beauty salon, and a Maxima supermarket. Several months before it opened, while construction was still taking place, a fire broke out in the supermarket, but nobody was injured.

On November 21, 2013, a fire alarm sounded at 4:21 p.m., and announcements were made to evacuate the building. Construction was taking place in the basement, and a welder was thought to be the cause of the alarm. Building security confirmed that there was no fire, so they turned off the alarm about 5:00 p.m. and did not carry out the evacuation. Some of the smaller shops, however, closed and customers and workers left the building, but they returned when they were told it was a false alarm. Many of Maxima's customers, however, remained in the store because they were not asked by employees to leave.

Before technicians could determine why the fire alarm had sounded, at 5:41, the roof collapsed in the Maxima supermarket. Because this was the peak shopping time as customers stopped on their way home from work, it was estimated that about 100 people were in the store, with 50 employees in the entire building. The roof collapsed over the lines of customers at the checkout counters, and over the dairy, alcohol, and household chemical aisles. Parts of the roof also fell onto cars parked outside.

Many of the people in the smaller shops were able to escape the building, as did some of the people in the supermarket. However, the collapse cut electrical power to the store, resulting in automatic locking of the front doors. Several people were trapped inside the front doors and had to break the glass to get out.

Within minutes, firefighters, police, and ambulances were on the scene. The rest of the roof seemed to be stable, so they quickly started a search-and-rescue operation, and pulled 20 people, most of those injured in the collapse, out of the rubble. Before they could complete the operation, at 7:04 p.m., another section of the roof collapsed, injuring 12 firefighters and killing three. After the second collapse, only five firefighters were allowed into the building at a time. Bulldozers and heavy cranes arrived to lift and remove rubble, which was as much as 8 feet (2.5 m) deep in places.

Before the evening was over the Latvian army had 110 soldiers on site to assist in the operation. Russia, Lithuania, and Estonia offered aid, but the government and rescue services believed they had the resources and experience to complete the rescue operation themselves. Searchers used thermal scanners to try to find survivors, but the concrete rubble was too thick to pick up heat signatures. Dogs were brought in, but they were unable to pick up human scents because of the alcohol and cleaning chemical containers that had broken open under the crush of debris. Rescuers would periodically call for silence and have relatives phone the missing so they could pinpoint victims by the ring tones. Police used surveillance video to map where shoppers were standing at the time of the collapse, to help rescuers find victims.

In the early morning of November 23, a day-and-a-half after the initial collapse, another firefighter was injured while clearing rubble. Later, at 5:52 p.m., another section of roof collapsed, shaking adjoining buildings. No one was injured, but by 7:00 p.m. all rescue efforts were stopped as the structural integrity of the remaining sections of roof was now compromised. Rescue personnel did not believe they would find anyone alive by this point, given the extent of injuries to the victims that were being recovered. Rescue operations resumed the next day, but no more victims were recovered.

The final death toll was 54, with 41 injured. It is not known how many people survived the initial collapse, as many of them left the scene during the initial chaos.

The mayor of Riga ordered an inspection to all building projects underway by the building company involved, Re&Re.

Official inquiries into the disaster began minutes after the initial collapse. Three theories were initially presented: faulty structural design, faulty construction practices, and construction that was underway at the time to build a green roof.

The investigation was hampered by the fact that the rest of the building still standing was considered too unsafe to enter. In April 2014, investigators were allowed into the building to inspect the damage and to perform controlled experiments on the building's remains. Much of the original evidence was destroyed in the third collapse. Investigators performed a controlled collapse of a remaining section of the roof, and set controlled fires to determine the load-bearing capacity of the supports and roof in the case of a fire, since a fire alarm preceded the collapse.

The controlled roof collapse test indicated the building's metal support structures were deformed before the roof was completed, and the supports eventually failed. This showed the roof was built improperly, and the collapse was not the result of some sudden change, but was caused by prolonged overloaded structures, exacerbated by metal fatigue.

A separate criminal inquiry was launched, and in January 2015 the first three suspects were named: a construction engineer, who failed to design the support structures properly; a design expert, who failed to notice this error and approved the design; and the architect.

Re&Re concluded that the collapse was the result of a design error. They claim the roof was designed to carry a load only one-third that which was necessary. Their report stated the collapse was due to a faulty calculation of the load-bearing capacity of the roof, and a faulty design of the steel structural supports.

Ivars Sergets, the owner of HND Grupa, the construction company responsible for building Zolitūde, claims that the collapse was the result of materials loaded onto weaker points of the roof. A green garden was being constructed on the roof at the time; plans called for 8–12 inches (20–30 cm) of topsoil and cobblestone paths connecting garden areas with benches. An underground car parking garage was also under construction in the basement. Sergets denies the garden had anything to do with the collapse, as the building had stood over two winters, and the weight of snow had been double the weight of the garden. He claimed that too many building materials were being stored on the roof. Later, he admitted that, although designs called for a single roof truss, the trusses were actually two pieces bolted together. Apparently the builders were unable to transport large single trusses to the construction site.

Engineers say that using two-piece trusses meant that the joint would bear most of the roof's weight. Video footage of the collapse shows that it failed exactly at the joints between the trusses. Other engineering studies have shown the bolts that held the bars together were too few, too small, and too weak. One of the firemen who responded to the disaster claimed that the bolts he saw had not broken, but had separated from the fasteners; this indicates the bolts were not designed to bear the weight of the roof.

Vilis Students, the vice director of the Latvian Fire Safety and Civil Defence College, who was part of the rescue party, reported that the concrete seemed fragile, as rescuers were able to break concrete debris apart using hammers and pliers.

The staff at Maxima supermarket told investigators the building had been unstable for a year. The foundation and roof had cracked and needed reinforcement. Extra roof supports had been added in the storage room, but were removed before the collapse. The fire alarm also sounded frequently, apparently because it could not distinguish between smoke and dust.

Another problem was uncovered by the inquiries. The subcontractor who installed the steel structural supports, instead of hiring a certified building inspector to oversee construction, forged the signature of an engineer, who was never paid, on construction documents.

Maxima employees, from the collapsed store as well as other stores, claimed they received inadequate safety instructions, fire escapes were routinely blocked, and if they left their duties, even to go to the toilet, their pay was reduced. Claims were also made that the company intimidated employees to keep them from reporting problems to authorities.

Political repercussions were quick to follow the collapse. On November 23, Latvian President Andris Bērziņš called the tragedy an act of mass murder and called for a criminal investigation led from abroad, as Latvian business interests were too intertwined with state politics to lead a fair investigation. On November 27, Latvian Prime Minister Valdis Dombrovskis took responsibility and resigned. Others blamed the abolishing of state building inspectors in 2009 during the economic downturn, because the sitting government believed it was a duplication of effort; municipal inspectors already performed the same duties. Riga's mayor suspended six members of the city's construction board who oversaw construction documents.

The mayor of Riga, Nils Ušakovs, says the remaining portion of the Maxima supermarket will be torn down and a memorial erected at the spot. The supermarket collapse was the worst disaster in Latvia since it regained independence from the Soviet Union in 1991.

41

Ufa Train Disaster

1989

USSR/Russia

"I have to say this: I believe we are being persecuted by these events — first one, then another. Many of them are caused by mismanagement, irresponsibility, disorganization." —Soviet President Mikhail S. Gorbachev

On June 4, 1989, a pipeline about 30 miles (50 km) from the city of Ufa in the Soviet Union began leaking. Pipeline operators noticed a drop in pressure that morning. Instead of searching for a cause, they increased pressure in the pipeline to keep the contents flowing. Liquid natural gas, mainly propane and butane, spilled from the pipeline, and a cloud of highly flammable gas formed about a half-mile (800 m) from the leak and settled in a gully along the Trans-Siberian Railway near the town of Asha in the Ural Mountains.

Two passenger trains carrying a total of 1,300 people were traveling in opposite directions on the nearby tracks. One was loaded with many children returning home to Novosibirsk in Siberia from a vacation resort near Sochi on the Black Sea; the other was loaded with children heading toward the resort.

Both engineers later reported they could smell the gas leak. Sparks from the wheels of the passing trains ignited the cloud, and a massive explosion occurred. The fireball expanded for a mile (1.6 km) and flattened trees within two-and-a-half miles (4 km) of the explosion; it could be seen 95 miles (153 km) away. The force of the blast has been estimated at 10 kilotons of TNT, almost as powerful as the nuclear blast over Hiroshima. It destroyed two locomotives and 37 train cars. Seven of them were burned to ash. Several dozen acres of forest were charred. Windows in Asha, eight miles (13 km) away were blown out by the explosion.

Witnesses reported that people "burned like matches" in the inferno. More than 100 ambulances responded, and a local helicopter training school provided air support to transport victims to hospitals. Military units searched the nearby forest for possible survivors.

Soviet figures report 575 deaths, with more than 800 injured, although the memorial at the site lists 675 names, and according to other accounts, 780 people were killed. It was the worst railroad disaster in Soviet history.

Rail traffic on the important Trans-Siberian Railway was disrupted until repairs could be made, as were energy supplies because of the ruptured pipeline. Soviet President Mikhail S. Gorbachev toured the disaster site and expressed frustration at lax Soviet safety standards, claiming that this was holding Russia back from her great potential.

News of the disaster was overshadowed by events at Tiananmen Square in Beijing, China, which had occurred a day earlier.

42

Doña Paz Ferry Sinking

1987

Philippines

"I went to a window to see what happened, and I saw the sea in flames. I shouted to my companions to get ready. 'There's a fire!' I said." —Paquito Osabel, survivor, who lost his sister and three nieces in the sinking

The passenger ferry *Himeyuri Maru* was built in Japan in 1963. While the ferry was used in Japanese waters, it had an official capacity of 608 persons. In 1975 it was sold to a Filipino operator of a fleet of passenger ferries, Sulpicio Lines, who renamed the ship the *Don Sulpicio*.

On June 5, 1979, while en route from Manila to Cebu, the *Don Sulpicio* was gutted by fire. Everyone was rescued, but the ship was beached and declared a total loss. Sulpicio Lines repurchased the ship from their underwriters; the *Don*

Sulpicio was refurbished, returned to service, and renamed the *Doña Paz*.

In December 1987, the *Doña Paz* sailed from Manila to Tacloban to Catbalogan to Manila, and then back, twice a week. On December 20, the ferry was near Dumali Point in the Tablas Strait off of Mindoro, and was due in to Manila at 4:00 a.m. the next morning. Many of the passengers were going to Manila for the Christmas holidays. Reports say the weather was clear but with choppy seas. At about 10:30 p.m., while most of the passengers slept, the *Doña Paz* collided with MT *Vector*, an oil tanker traveling from Bataan to Masbate. The *Vector* carried 8,800 barrels of petroleum products, including gasoline.

The collision ignited a massive fire on the *Vector*, which spread quickly to the *Doña Paz*. Survivors recall feeling the crash and explosion, which caused panic to break out among the passengers. Raging flames covered the surface of the sea surrounding both ships. The lights went out on the *Doña Paz*. No life vests could be found; it was later determined that the life vest lockers were locked. Crew members were panicking along with the passengers, and no crew members gave instructions or attempted to organize the passengers to escape the ship. Survivors were forced to jump into the flaming waters surrounding the ship as both ships sank. The *Doña Paz* sank within two hours, and the *Vector* within four, into shark-infested waters 1,788 feet (545 m) deep.

It was eight hours before Philippine authorities learned of the sinkings, and eight more hours for search-and-rescue operations to begin. Another passenger ship in the area, the *Don Eusebio*, circled the area for seven hours but could find no trace of survivors or debris.

Only 26 survivors were pulled from the water by a passing merchant vessel, most of them with serious burns. Twenty-four were from the *Doña Paz* (all passengers; no crew survived), and two, who claimed to be sleeping when the ships collided, were from the *Vector*. It would be far more difficult to determine how many had died.

According to Sulpicio Lines, the passenger capacity of the *Doña Paz* was 1,424. The company announced that the official passenger manifest recorded 1,493 passengers and crew. The company revised those numbers within days, saying 1,583 passengers and 58 crew were aboard. Sources from Sulpicio Lines, however, reported that extra tickets were usually illegally purchased on board at a cheaper rate, and those passengers, as well as holders of complimentary tickets and nonpaying passengers under the age of four would not be listed on the official manifest.

Survivors claim that many passengers were sleeping in corridors, or on floors or the decks, and many cots were set up on which three or four people were sleeping. Of the first 21 bodies to be identified, only one was on the manifest. Of the 24 surviving passengers, only five were on the manifest. It was estimated that perhaps 3,000 to 4,000 people had been on the *Doña Paz* at the time of the disaster.

On December 28, a local official claimed that at least 2,000 passengers were not on the manifest, based on the list of names of those reported missing. In February 1988, the Philippine National Bureau of Investigation claimed that at least 3,099 passengers and 59 crew had been aboard, putting the death toll from the *Doña Paz* at 3,134. A 1999 presidential task force estimated that, based on settlement claims, there were 4,375 fatalities on the *Doña Paz* and 11 from the *Vector* crew, making the final death toll 4,386. These estimates make the sinking of the *Doña Paz* the deadliest peacetime maritime disaster in history.

Sulpicio Lines was willing to compensate families US$472 for each victim.

The official investigation was led by the Philippine Coast Guard. The inquiry determined that the *Doña Paz* carried no radio, and only one apprentice crew member of the *Doña Paz* was monitoring the bridge when the collision took place. The other officers were drinking beer or watching television; the captain was watching a movie on his Betamax in his cabin. It also became known that the *Vector* was operating without a license, a lookout, or a properly qualified master.

The Board of Marine Inquiry cleared Sulpicio Lines of any fault in the disaster. The Supreme Court of the Philippines ruled in 1999 that the owners of the *Vector* were liable for the collision.

Other Sulpicio Lines ferries have been involved in accidents since the sinking of the *Doña Paz*. The *Doña Marilyn* capsized when hit by huge waves during Typhoon Ruby in 1988, less than a year later; hundreds perished. In 1998 the *Princess of the Orient* sank, with 70 dead and 80 missing. The *Princess of the World* caught fire in 2005; all of the passengers were rescued.

43

New London School Explosion

1937

Texas, USA

"I could not believe what I was seeing. That beautiful two story school building was completely shattered, only a few walls standing, and they were at a crazy angle. I went over the fence and approached what had been the school building. What I saw that day is still impressed in my mind. All I could see was mangled steel and concrete with small bodies everywhere. I suppose I was in shock, I thought I could not stand to go in there." —Howard Coleman, who arrived at the scene after the explosion

In the mid-1930s, despite the ongoing Great Depression, the town of London (now New London) in northeastern Texas was enjoying a booming local economy. In 1930, oil had been discovered in Rusk County, and local spending was in boom mode.

The London School District was one of the richest districts in the country at the time. In 1932, it built London School at a cost of $1 million ($15.75 million in 2009 dollars). The large school was constructed of steel and concrete. The school's football stadium was the first one in the state to have electric lights.

The original architectural plans called for a boiler and steam distribution system to heat the building, but the school board overruled the plans and decided to install 72 gas heaters throughout the building. In 1937, in order to save money, the board canceled their contract for natural gas and had plumbers tap into a residue gas line owned by Parade Gasoline Company instead. The residual gas was natural gas that was extracted with oil, and was seen as a waste product and often flared off. This type of gas varies in quality from hour to hour. Since the gas was considered waste, oil companies looked the other way as others tapped into the gas lines. This practice was common in the area.

Untreated natural gas is colorless and odorless, so it is difficult to detect. The gas line connecting the tapped line to the school had been improperly installed, and gas leaked into a long crawlspace of some 64,000 cubic feet (1,812 cubic meters) under the school. Plans to ventilate the crawlspace were never implemented. Students had been complaining of headaches for a while, but the cause was never investigated.

On Thursday, March 18, 1937, first through fourth graders had been dismissed on schedule. Shortly after 3:00 p.m., about 10 minutes before school was to be dismissed for the day, one of the instructors turned on an electric sander. The sander's switch created a spark, and the gas in the crawlspace under the school ignited.

About 600 students and 40 teachers were in the building at the time. Witnesses saw the school walls bulge out and the roof lift off into the air and come crashing down. Most of the school collapsed. The explosion blew a two-ton piece of concrete through the air and onto a parked car, crushing it. At least one student thought that Hitler had bombed their school.

The intense boom of the explosion served as an alarm to everyone for miles. Many parents were attending a PTA meeting at the time in a nearby building on the school campus, and they immediately rushed over to rescue students. Within minutes, many of the town's residents had arrived and starting digging through the rubble for survivors, in many cases with their bare hands. Workers from nearby oil fields rushed to the site with heavy equipment and cutting torches.

Within 15 minutes, word had spread via telephone and telegraph lines. Outside aid from the Texas Rangers, Texas National Guard, and Highway Patrol quickly reached the town. Medical response teams were sent from Dallas.

An Associated Press reporter estimated that 2,000 rescue workers were present and dug through the rubble that night in the rain, clearing the site of five million pounds (2,268 metric tons) of bricks and steel. Within 17 hours of the explosion, the site had been cleared. The bodies were taken to makeshift morgues; most were so mutilated they could only be identified by personal belongings or the clothing they wore. One child's body was found entangled in nearby electric lines, 30 feet (9 m) in the air. A casket company in Dallas went to around-the-clock shifts so enough caskets would be available.

News reporters were dispatched to the town, but were quickly pressed into the relief effort. On one of his first assignments for United Press, Walter Cronkite arrived in London. Although he later covered stories in World War II including the Nuremburg Trials, decades later he said, "I did nothing in my studies nor in my life to prepare me for a story of the magnitude of that New London tragedy, nor has any story since that awful day equaled it." He remained at the scene for four days, covering the disaster and then the funerals.

Of the approximately 640 people in the building at the time, only 130 escaped serious injury. The death toll was at least 295 students and teachers, making it the deadliest school disaster in American history. Even German Chancellor Adolf Hitler paid his respects to the town by telegram.

Not all of the campus buildings were destroyed. The gymnasium building survived and was quickly partitioned into classrooms so classes could resume 10 days after the disaster. A new school was built on the site in 1939.

Experts determined that the connection to the residue gas line was faulty and was the root cause of the disaster. In response, within weeks Texas required that thiols, which have a foul odor, be added to natural gas so that the smell can alert people to a gas leak. Soon, that requirement spread worldwide.

Because the accident was seen as an engineering failure, the Texas State Legislature established the Texas State Board of Registration for Professional Engineers, so that anyone practicing engineering had to be licensed.

The big question remained: why had a school district with plenty of wealth risk student's lives to save $3,000 a year on heating fuel? Petroleum experts considered this free natural gas to be too dangerous for commercial use. The school district and Parade Gasoline Company were sued for the disaster, but the court ruled that neither were responsible. The school superintendent was threatened with lynching and was forced to resign, despite the fact that he had lost a son in the blast.

The townsfolk collectively tried to put the disaster behind them by rarely speaking of it. Many survivors attribute this to a collective guilt over the death of a substantial portion of the town's children in order to save a few dollars. It wasn't until 1977 that the town hosted a reunion for survivors and their families.

A monument to the victims of the blast was erected in 1939. The 34-foot (10.4-m) high granite cenotaph lists the names of each victim.

44

Shiloh Baptist Church Panic

1902

Alabama, USA

"NEGRO DEAD NUMBER 115. NO WHITE PEOPLE KILLED IN THE BIRMINGHAM PANIC. —New York Times headline, November 21, 1902

In 1902, the Shiloh Baptist Church was the largest black church in Birmingham, Alabama. On September 19, approximately 3,000 crowded into the church (with more outside) as Booker T. Washington addressed the National Convention of Negro Baptists.

Washington, born into slavery, had become the leader of the African American community, promoting education, political involvement, and economic advancement instead of confrontation. As a speaker, he regularly attracted large crowds. The pews at Shiloh Baptist Church were filled, and the aisles and stairways were packed with those unable to find seats.

After he concluded his remarks at Shiloh Baptist Church, according to Washington, there was a scream behind him. He said the next day that a Birmingham man had stepped on the toes of a delegate to the convention from Baltimore, who resented it and made a motion as if he was drawing a gun, causing a woman to scream. Other accounts say that there was a dispute between the visitor from Baltimore and the choir leader over an unoccupied seat. Regardless, a member of the choir yelled "Fight!" The audience

226

understood the shout as "Fire!", and they rose and started stampeding toward the door.

One of the ministers rose, and urged the people not to panic. He repeated the word "Quiet!" several times, which, in the chaos, the congregation again heard as "Fire!" and rushed even faster for the door. People scrambled over the pews and fought their way into the aisles. Some fell and were trampled to death; others fainted in the chaos and were also trampled to death. Women and children screamed in horror. The throng was so thick that several men tried to walk across the heads in the crowd to get out.

Booker T. Washington started the choir singing, in order to calm the crowd. Some in the crowd joined in.

Outside the front doors was a staircase that descended to street level, which was about 15 feet (4.56 m) lower. Brick walls blocked escape to the sides of the stairway. When the first people to escape the church reached the top of the stairs, the crush of people threw them forward, down the stairs. They were unable to get up before more people were pushed on top of them, and in short order there was a pile of people 10 feet (3 m) high trying to extricate themselves from the writhing pile. More than 20 people suffocated under the pile, which blocked the exit for about 1,500 people still trying to escape the church.

A policeman had been stationed at the doorway, but he was trapped against the wall in the stampede. Most of his clothing was torn from his body. His legs were crushed, but he survived.

Two men who had managed to escape before the crush of bodies on the stairs called in a fire alarm. When the Fire Department and Police Department arrived, they pushed back a growing crowd of onlookers in front of the church, and then started pulling people out of the pile and out of the jammed doorway. When the dead bodies and the doorway were cleared, another mass of people started pouring out of the church. Many of them fell down the long stairway, suffering broken bones and internal injuries. Some of the injured managed to get away from the church, but collapsed and died in the weeds of the adjoining vacant lot.

With the stampede now over, the church was quickly cleared of bodies in about an hour. Physicians who lived nearby came to render aid, but about 15 of the injured died before they could receive medical treatment. It took three hours for ambulances to haul away the dead.

In all, 115 people died that day. Almost all of the victims were either crushed to death or suffocated. Identification of the victims was complicated by the fact that many were visitors to the city for the convention.

In 1927, the church was demolished to make way for a Veterans Administration Hospital.

45

Palace of the Grand Master Explosion

1856

Greece

The ancient island city of Rhodes, Greece is best known for the giant statue, the Colossus of Rhodes, one of the Seven Wonders of the Ancient World. Near the site of the ancient statue was the Palace of the Grand Master of the Knights of Rhodes, a medieval castle, which sat on the highest point in Rhodes. When the Ottoman Empire captured the island of Rhodes around 1522, the palace became a command center and fortress.

In 1856, the Palace of the Grand Master and the neighboring church, the Church of St. John, were used for ammunition storage, although it was still open to the public. The large complex could hold thousands of people.

On April 3, 1856, a storm approached the island and thousands of people sought shelter at the palace. The church bells were rung; the townspeople foolishly believed that ringing church bells could disrupt the formation of lightning. Nevertheless, a bolt of lightning hit the palace, setting off a fire. The fire spread to the explosives, which detonated in a massive blast. The palace was reduced to rubble, and about 4,000 people in and around the palace were killed, in what may be the deadliest lightning strike in history.

Italy took control of Rhodes during the Italo-Turkish War in 1912. The palace remained a rubble pile for almost 80 years. It sat in ruins until it was rebuilt between 1937 and

1940. It was then used as a holiday residence for Vittorio Emmanuele III, the King of Italy, and then for Benito Mussolini, the fascist dictator of Italy during World War II. In 1948, the Dodecanese Islands were transferred from Italy to Greece as part of the Paris Peace Treaties. The palace was converted into the Byzantine Museum, which millions of tourists have visited in the years since. The medieval Old Town of Rhodes is now a UNESCO World Heritage Site.

46

Peshtigo Fire

1871

Wisconsin, USA

"Once in water up to our necks, I thought we would, at least be safe from fire, but it was not so; the flames darted over the river as they did over land, the air was full of them, or rather the air itself was on fire. Our heads were in continual danger." —Rev. Peter Pernin, survivor

The deadliest firestorm in history, even worse than the Kursha-2 firestorm, took place in and around Peshtigo, Wisconsin, on October 8, 1871. Clear-cutting of the forested land on the west side of Green Bay was widespread in 1871. The lumber that was harvested was sent south to build the growing cities of Milwaukee and Chicago. The Northwestern Rail Road was being built along the west shore from Green Bay through Peshtigo to Menomonee, Michigan, and the right-of-way was cut and burned for expediency. Farmers were slashing and burning forests so they could plant crops to feed the growing settlements of eastern Wisconsin. Piles of branches and sawdust left behind by lumbermen provided plenty of wildfire fuel.

The summer and autumn of 1871 were extremely hot and dry in the American Midwest. Practically no substantial rain had fallen in the area for three months. The trees and underbrush were tinder dry. Small forest fires had been burning for weeks, covering the area in a smoky haze. One of these fires had been fought just outside Peshtigo on September 24. The Green Island Light, in Green Bay just east of Peshtigo, was kept burning day and night to guide seamen safely through the smoke. Despite that, the schooner *George L. Newman* was wrecked offshore, without loss of life.

By October 8, numerous fires were burning around Peshtigo. Railway workers continued to slash-and-burn to extend the tracks toward Peshtigo, ignoring warnings about the tinder dry conditions. On October 8, a strong cold front moved in from the west. Strong winds whipped the fires into a massive conflagration. A firestorm developed, and modern research shows that a firenado formed and moved through the town between 9:00 and 10:00 p.m., crossing the Peshtigo River to burn both sides of town. People, houses, and rail cars were thrown into the air by the intense firenado winds. (See Chapter 37 for an explanation of firestorms and firenados and how they form.)

Harper's Weekly illustration (1871) (Image courtesy of Wisconsin Electronic Reader)

Once the first house in town burst into flames, survivors claim that within one minute the entire town was burning. Survivors escaped the flames by jumping into the Peshtigo River; some of them died of hypothermia in the cold water.

Those who weren't so lucky burst into flames as they ran to escape the firenado. Survivors who sought refuge in the Peshtigo River reported that for an hour, the heat was so intense they could only bring their head out of the water for a few seconds at a time. Many of them suffered severe burns to their head and face. Nothing could be done to stop the advancing flames, and within three hours, the fire had swept through the entire town, obliterating it almost completely.

No building in Peshtigo survived. The pail and tub factory, less than a year old and one of the largest in the U.S., and an extensive wood mill which manufactured doors and blinds, were not only lost, but provided more fuel for the fire. The Peshtigo Company's sawmill had numerous shops where cars, logging sleds, and other implements for harvesting wood and milling lumber were also lost.

At least 400 died at the Peshtigo Company's boarding house. The nearby community of Sugar Bush, home to about 300 families, suffered a loss of about 80% of its inhabitants. Large numbers of cattle and horses also burned.

The 1870 census had reported 1,749 people living in Peshtigo. Local records burned in the fire, making a full accounting of the toll almost impossible. A government report on the disaster two years later listed 1,182 dead or missing. More than 350 were buried in a mass grave because no relatives survived to claim the bodies. The Peshtigo Fire was the deadliest wildfire in American history.

The massive firestorm spread up and down the west shoreline of Green Bay in Wisconsin and Michigan. Another fire erupted on the east side of the bay, burning much of the Door Peninsula. The fire destroyed twelve towns and consumed more than 1,875 square miles (4,860 square kilometers, 1.2 million acres) of woodland, about twice the size of Rhode Island. In many hamlets and settlements, most, if not all of the structures burned to the ground, with only handfuls of survivors.

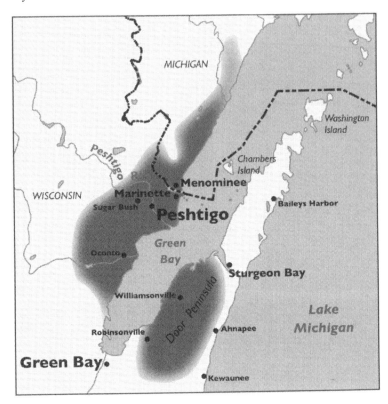

In the town of Robinson (now Champion) on the Door Peninsula, nuns, farmers, and their families sought refuge in a chapel. While they prayed to the Virgin Mary for protection, the chapel was surrounded by flames. The chapel and its occupants survived unharmed, and a miracle was credited. Today, the Shrine of Our Lady of Good Help marks the location of the original chapel and is a popular destination for those on religious pilgrimages.

In Williamson, 55 charred bodies were found at the burned mill; only 12 survivors were found.

Women and children from the villages of Marinette, Wisconsin, and Menominee, Michigan, sought refuge from the spreading inferno on steamers, which took them out into Green Bay, while all of the men stayed behind, trying to save the towns from total destruction.

The Peshtigo area was not the only area which burned on the night of October 8, 1871. Wildfires also destroyed Holland, Manistee, and Port Huron in Michigan, as well as much of eastern Michigan's thumb-shaped peninsula. The following day, Urbana, Illinois, was destroyed by fire, and three days after that, Windsor, Ontario, Canada burned.

Farther south the same night as the Peshtigo Fire, fire consumed the city of Chicago. The Great Chicago Fire killed as many as 300 people and is considered one of America's great disasters, but the death toll is dwarfed by the Peshtigo disaster the same night. Because Chicago was a fast-growing, economically-important city, word of that disaster spread quickly, while it took Americans longer to learn of the other fire disasters that night, partly because the telegraph line to Green Bay had burned before a distress message could be sent.

Survivors over a large swath of Wisconsin and Michigan had nothing left; in many cases even their clothing was burned off their bodies. Without food, shelter, or clothing, they were destitute and in need of immediate assistance. Wisconsinites responded as soon as they heard about the disaster with ships and trains full of relief supplies. The rest of the country was reading sensational headlines about the Great Chicago Fire, and focused their relief efforts there. The Great Chicago Fire lives on in American historical lore, but the Peshtigo Fire has been largely forgotten.

Peshtigo was rebuilt, and today visitors can view monuments dedicated to the disaster, the Peshtigo Fire

Cemetery, and the Peshtigo Fire Museum. However, the town never fully recovered from the great fire. Before the firestorm, the town was quickly becoming a major lumber port town on the Great Lakes, but when Peshtigo was destroyed, most economic and port activity moved to nearby Marinette, Wisconsin, and Menominee, Michigan, which are today the largest towns in the region.

The American and British military studied the Peshtigo Fire in detail during World War II. They sought to learn how to recreate firestorm conditions during bombing campaigns in Germany and Japan. The military used the information they learned to plan the firebombings of Dresden and Tokyo in 1945, which resulted in the deaths of nearly 25,000 in Dresden and possibly more than 100,000 in Tokyo. The death toll in these two cities exceeded that of the atomic bombings of Hiroshima and Nagasaki.

47

Lagos Armory Explosion

2002

Nigeria

"I was at work in the office with my 3-year-old kid at Ogba, about six or seven kilometres from the military cantonment, when it happened — I thought the building was going to collapse! The vibrations were so great and I was surprised the office windows didn't smash. It felt like several earthquakes were going on all at the same time. It was real scary... It was almost like our own Sept 11." — Kayode Akomolafe

The city of Lagos, Nigeria, is one of the world's largest, and fastest-growing, cities. Starting with the 1970s Nigerian oil boom, the city's population has quickly climbed to somewhere around 15 to 20 million.

In 2002, Ikeja was a large military base and storage facility north of the city center near the airport. On its grounds, the Nigerian military stored high-caliber munitions. Many soldiers and their families also lived in the compound.

On the afternoon of January 27, 2002, in a street market adjacent to the military base, a fire broke out. By around 6:00 p.m., the fire had spread to the main munitions storage area, resulting in a huge explosion. Many of the base's soldiers, staff, and their families were killed in the blast.

The shockwave shattered windows more than nine miles (15 km) away in the city center and could be felt 31 miles (50 km) away. The blast flattened many buildings in the densely-packed neighboring residential area, trapping residents inside. Damaged cooking appliances from the shockwave and collapsing buildings started new fires.

The explosion also threw unexploded ordnance into the sky. As exploding shells, grenades, and bullets rained down on the city, people attempted to flee the area. Some residents believed that a military coup was taking place (military rule had just ended a few years earlier in 1999). The streets became increasingly congested, and a stampede developed by the panicking survivors. People jumped from burning high-rise buildings; others died trying to cross a busy Ikeja highway.

Many survivors attempted to seek refuge in a large banana plantation. A canal separated the plantation from the burning city; but water hyacinth completely covered the canal. Panicked people could not see the water, and, as the fleeing crowd surged forward, hundreds fell into the water. As more and more people fell into the canal, the people on the bottom were crushed and drowned. At least 600 people, many of them children, died in the canal.

The city's emergency services could not deal with death and destruction on such a massive scale. Fires spread unchecked as there were not enough firefighting crews or water. The hospitals were so overwhelmed that, even if survivors made it to an undamaged medical facility, they often waited untreated for hours. The military was unprepared to respond, as many of its personnel had perished in the initial blast. They did not arrive in large numbers until the following day.

A large area of the northern suburbs of Lagos continued to burn through the night, gutting homes, offices, shopping centers, and schools. Secondary explosions continued until the next afternoon. By that evening, most fires were under control, and residents began to return to search for loved ones. It would be another day before the fires were extinguished.

The government and military took to the airwaves to assure residents that the explosions were the result of an accident, not an attempt by the military to stage another coup.

Besides the deaths at the canal, hundreds of others had died in the blast, trapped in fires, by falling munitions, or trampled by the fleeing crowds. Although it is impossible to know the final death toll, the Red Cross claimed 1,000 bodies were recovered. Others were reported missing and never found. The generally accepted death toll stands at about 1,100. Upwards of 5,000 people were injured, and 20,000 were displaced from their homes. At least 12,000 returned to find their homes destroyed.

Nigerian President Olusegun Obasanjo visited Ikeja the day after the blast and demanded an explanation. He even climbed up onto the hood of his car to calm the crowds. Why had the military kept such a huge, poorly maintained munitions dump inside the city, without regard for public safety? It soon came out that an explosion had occurred in 2001 on the base, and the civilian government had subsequently ordered the base be maintained properly or decommissioned; it never happened. Residents placed the blame on the military, saying they had ruined the country during nearly three decades of military rule, and had now destroyed their city with their carelessness. The military base commander issued a short apology for the blast and blamed the government, sparking fears that the explosion would result in another military coup.

The Red Cross and Red Crescent provided aid to thousands over the course of the next few weeks, as many people had lost their homes and their livelihoods. Survivors were again evacuated from Ikeja so that the military could remove the large remaining stockpile of unexploded munitions from the base and scattered around city streets.

48

Galveston Hurricane

1900

Texas, USA

> *"... the force of the waves acted as a battering ram
> against which it was impossible for any building to stand
> for any length of time, and at 8:30 p.m. my residence
> went down with about fifty persons who had sought it for
> safety, and all but eighteen were hurled into eternity.
> Among the lost was my wife, who never rose above the
> water after the wreck of the building. I was nearly
> drowned and became unconscious, but recovered through
> being crushed by timbers and found myself clinging to my
> youngest child, who had gone down with myself and wife.
> Mr. J. L. Cline [his brother] joined me five minutes later
> with my other two children, and with them and a woman
> and child we picked up from the raging waters, we drifted
> for three hours, landing 300 yards from where we
> started."* —Isaac Cline, Galveston section director, U.S.
> Weather Bureau

In late August, 1900, a tropical wave formed off the west coast of Africa and spawned a small tropical disturbance, which, in typical fashion each summer and autumn, moved west across the Atlantic Ocean. On August 27, about 1,000 miles (1,600 km) east of the Windward Islands, a passing ship's captain noted the unsettled weather. By August 30, the storm system, now a tropical depression, passed the Leeward Islands of the northeastern Caribbean Sea, heading toward Puerto Rico and Hispaniola.

Weather forecasting in 1900 was at best an educated guess. U.S. Weather Bureau officials were loath to use the words "hurricane" or "tornado" in their forecasts in order to prevent panic, and because they simply did not understand that much about weather patterns and forecasting.

The Bureau began to take notice on September 1 and reported a "storm of moderate intensity (not a hurricane)" to the southeast of Cuba. On September 3, this storm made landfall in western Cuba and two days later was in the Florida Straits.

The Weather Bureau predicted the storm would cross the Florida Peninsula and continue northeastward back into the Atlantic. Cuban meteorologists insisted the hurricane would head west across the Gulf of Mexico and make landfall somewhere in Texas. The U.S. Weather Bureau ignored the Cuban reports.

The conditions for tropical storm development and strengthening in the Gulf of Mexico were in place. The water was as warm as bathwater because there had been little cloud cover for weeks.

On September 6, the storm was north of Key West, Florida. The next morning, the Weather Bureau office in New Orleans, Louisiana reported heavy damage along the Louisiana and Mississippi coasts. In response, the Bureau issued storm warnings along the Gulf coast from Pensacola, Florida to Galveston, Texas. That afternoon, large swells were rolling across the Gulf of Mexico, signs of a major storm. A ship leaving New Orleans entered the hurricane that afternoon; the captain estimated winds at 100 mph (160 kph), the equivalent of a Category 2 hurricane using today's Saffir-Simpson Hurricane Scale. The Weather Bureau at this point was still expecting the hurricane to move north and back out into the Atlantic. In fact, it was heading straight for

Galveston, Texas.

In 1900, Galveston was a boom town. With 37,778 residents, it was the fourth-largest city in Texas. Because it was located on a barrier island at the entrance to the natural harbor of Galveston Bay, it was the center of trade for the area. It was the state's up-and-coming city. The problem was that the highest point in the city was only 8.7 feet (2.7 m) above sea level, and the town had been built on a sandbar. To make matters worse, as the city grew, sand dunes along the shore were removed and used to fill low areas; this destruction of the natural barrier dunes removed what little protection there was from rising water.

In 1875, a strong hurricane struck Indianola, on Matagorda Bay southwest of Galveston. Indianola, a boom town itself and the second most important port in Texas after Galveston, was nearly destroyed. Indianola was rebuilt, but eleven years later another hurricane caused significant damage; most residents gave up and left.

Some residents of Galveston pointed at the destruction of Indianola and realized that hurricanes were a real threat. They proposed that a seawall be constructed to protect the city, but the city's government, as well as a majority of its population, didn't see the need, and the project was never launched.

Since the founding of Galveston in 1839, eleven hurricanes had hit the city, but the city had weathered them all. Residents of the city were convinced that no strong hurricanes could strike the city, because none had so far. This belief was strengthened by Isaac Cline, the Galveston Weather Bureau director. Despite the destruction of Indianola, Cline publicly stated that it was impossible for strong hurricanes to strike the western Gulf of Mexico. He argued that a seawall to protect Galveston was unnecessary.

243

The Weather Bureau, whose task was to issue forecasts and public warnings in the U.S., issued warnings to the Galveston office from the central office in Washington, D.C. on September 4. They warned that a tropical storm had moved over Cuba, but had already begun a curve to the right, making it appear that the storm would continue arcing to the east and pass over Florida into the Atlantic. However, a high-pressure system in the southeast U.S. was blocking movement to the north. Cuban forecasters continued to warn that the hurricane would strike the Texas coast and move inland, probably near San Antonio.

By Saturday, September 8, there were signs that a tropical storm was heading toward Galveston. A steady wind out of the northeast was blowing. Large swells were forming on the Gulf and striking the city's beaches. But few people left the city for higher ground.

That morning, a train from Houston to Galveston found tracks washed out; passengers had to be transferred to another train on parallel tracks to make it into the city. Debris had washed onto the tracks in places. Another train on its way from Beaumont was waiting on the Bolivar Peninsula, north of Galveston across the entrance to the harbor; a ferry would take the train and its passengers to Galveston Island. When the ferry finally arrived, high seas prevented the ferry captain from docking. The train's engineer tried to go back the way he had come, but by then the tracks had been washed away by the pounding surf. Ten people on the train joined the 200 residents of the town of Port Bolivar taking refuge at the Point Bolivar Lighthouse. The 85 passengers who remained with the train perished when the storm surge washed over the train.

By that afternoon, September 8, 1900, the hurricane was bearing down at full force on the city of Galveston. By the time people realized what was happening, it was too late to flee the city. A storm surge of more than 15 feet (4.6 m) washed over the entire island. As the storm surge poured in from the Gulf, northerly winds pushed the water of Galveston Bay into the city from that direction.

The last message to be sent from the city before the telegraph lines blew down was a report from Isaac Cline, reporting that half of the city was underwater. The bridges connecting Galveston to the mainland were soon destroyed, along with the telegraph lines, so there was no way to call the mainland for help.

Buildings were knocked off their foundations, and the pounding surf pulverized them. A railroad trestle that ran along the beach was broken up and, along with the multitude of smashed houses, formed a long wall of debris. The debris wall smashed everything in its path as it moved farther inland with each wave, riding the rising storm surge.

Residents were forced to the second floors, attics, and even roofs of their homes to avoid the storm surge. Ten Sisters and 90 children at St. Mary's Orphans Asylum along the beach died when the orphanage buildings collapsed and were washed away; three children survived. The wall of debris crushed by the surf snaked through the town and was two stories high in places. St. Mary's Infirmary, the town's hospital, still stood, but there was no food or water. Two of the hospital's Sisters scoured the town for water-soaked food, dried it over a fire built in the street, and served it to survivors.

The highest recorded wind speed was measured shortly after 6:00 p.m. at 100 mph (160 kph). Shortly after that measurement was taken, the Weather Bureau's anemometer was blown away. Maximum winds were estimated at 120 mph (190 kph), but later studies suggest it was a Category 4 hurricane at landfall with winds of approximately 145 mph (233 kph).

The Weather Bureau office measured the barometric pressure at 28.48 inches of mercury (964.4 millibars), such a low air pressure measurement that observers believed it was an error. Modern studies indicate the pressure actually reached 27.49 inches (935.7 millibars).

Isaac Cline's house was destroyed and his wife killed; of the 40 people who sought refuge in his well-built house, more than 20 died.

The eye of the hurricane passed over Galveston Island just west of the city, putting Galveston in the right front quadrant of the hurricane, where the storm surge is the greatest. By 11:00 p.m., winds were diminishing, and by Sunday morning, skies were clear.

The next morning, after the storm had passed, the *Pherabe*, one of the only ships to survive the storm at the Galveston wharf, made its way to Texas City, on the west side of Galveston Bay. Six messengers from Galveston were aboard. They made it to Houston at 3:00 a.m. on September 10, and telegraphed Texas Governor Joseph D. Sayers and U.S. President William McKinley to report that Galveston was in ruins. They estimated 500 dead; this number was considered a gross exaggeration.

In the meantime, residents of Houston, well aware that a significant storm had just blown through, set out by rail and by ship to reach Galveston. When they arrived, they found the city almost completely obliterated. Only a handful of sturdily-built mansions in the Strand District had survived the storm surge. Many victims had drowned or were crushed by the waves of debris. Many who survived were trapped under the rubble. As rescuers walked among the debris trying to rescue survivors, they could hear screams coming from under the piles of wreckage. Some couldn't be reached and died days after the storm struck.

Estimates of the death toll range from 6,000 to 12,000; the generally accepted number is 8,000, or about 20% of the city's population. At least 30,000 were homeless. It was the deadliest hurricane, and in fact the deadliest natural disaster of any kind, in American history. It was the third deadliest Atlantic hurricane in history, following the Great Hurricane of 1780 (20,000–22,000 dead in the eastern Caribbean) and Hurricane Mitch in 1998 (nearly 19,000 dead in Central America). More people were killed in the Galveston Hurricane than in the more than 300 tropical storms and hurricanes that have struck the U.S. since 1900 combined.

There were so many bodies, it was impossible to bury them on the small island. Bodies were loaded onto barges, weighted down, and dumped at sea. When these bodies began to wash up on the city's beaches shortly thereafter, huge funeral pyres were constructed on the beaches; these pyres burned day and night for several weeks as more bodies were pulled out of the wreckage of the city. City officials provided free whiskey to the men hired to collect and burn the dead. Nearly all of the surviving men were enlisted to rescue people and dispose of the dead bodies.

More than 3,600 buildings had been destroyed, and 97.5% of the remaining homes were damaged. Surplus U.S. Army tents were hastily put up along the beach for shelter. Many survivors used the smashed lumber that covered the island to construct shelters.

The hurricane continued on as a tropical storm (with winds measured at 39–50 mph, 63–80 kph) far inland, crossing over Wisconsin and Lake Michigan, where tropical storms only hit once every 50 years. It dropped four inches (10 cm) of rain in Milwaukee, Wisconsin. Winds reached 72 mph (116 kph) in Chicago and 78 mph (126 kph) in Buffalo, New York. In New York, 65 mph (105 kph) winds struck; a falling sign pole killed one. It passed north of Halifax, Nova Scotia on September 12 and moved into the North Atlantic, where it destroyed a fleet of fishing boats off the coast of Newfoundland. The total charted path of the storm was more than 4,000 miles (6,400 km) long.

The call went out for a more thorough understanding of hurricanes in particular and weather patterns in general. The Weather Bureau needed to better understand these storms so they could be tracked and people could be warned ahead of time, so a disaster of this magnitude would never happen again.

Before the hurricane, Galveston was the center of commercial activity in the region. Now it seemed too risky to make major investments in shipping and manufacturing facilities on Galveston Island. After the storm, as rebuilding commenced, economic activity shifted inland to Houston. An oil boom in Houston, and then the dredging of the Houston Ship Channel, cemented Houston's place as the major commercial center of the region.

The rebuilding of Galveston included improving the city to prevent another calamity like this from happening again. Using sand dredged out of the Galveston Ship Channel, the city was raised by as much as 17 feet (5.2 m). Enough sand was poured on the city to fill a million dump trucks. More than 2,100 buildings were raised, including St. Patrick's Church, weighing 3,000 tons (2,722 metric tons). Everything had to be raised: sewer lines, gas lines, water mains, and entire buildings. It took seven years to raise the city.

A 17-foot (5.2-m) high seawall was constructed along three miles (4.8 km) of the beach; it was later extended to a length of 10 miles (16 km). An all-weather bridge was built to the mainland.

Galveston didn't have long to wait to see if the improvements made a difference. In August 1915, a similar hurricane struck Galveston following essentially the same track. Only 53 people on Galveston Island died this time.

The recently-formed American Red Cross, led by Clara Barton, established a new orphanage in Galveston and helped acquire building materials for the rebuilding process. It raised money to do this by selling photographs of the damage the storm had caused. Barton said her Red Cross workers "grew pale and ill" because of the human toll taken by the hurricane. Galveston was the last disaster at which Barton would personally assist.

49

Chernobyl Nuclear Meltdown

1986

USSR/Ukraine

"We arrived there at 10 or 15 minutes to two in the morning... We saw graphite scattered about. Misha asked: 'What is graphite?' I kicked it away. But one of the fighters on the other truck picked it up. 'It's hot,' he said. The pieces of graphite were of different sizes, some big, some small enough to pick up. . . We didn't know much about radiation. Even those who worked there had no idea. There was no water left in the trucks. Misha filled the cistern and we aimed the water at the top. Then those boys who died went up to the roof... They went up the ladder... and I never saw them again." —Vladimir Shevchenko, Russian filmmaker, who accompanied firefighters onto the roof of the burning reactor wearing only a surgical mask for protection. He died from radiation poisoning a few weeks later, but his name is not on the official casualty list.

Perhaps the Chernobyl nuclear accident in the U.S.S.R. in 1986 has changed the world more than any other incident described in this book. The accident occurred on April 26, 1986, during a test in Reactor 4 at the Chernobyl Nuclear Power Plant in Ukrainian SSR (then part of the U.S.S.R., now the country of Ukraine).

Chernobyl is the worst nuclear power plant accident in history in terms of casualties and the cost of damage and cleanup. It is one of only two Level 7 events ever recorded on the International Nuclear Event Scale, the highest classification of disaster. The other was the Fukushima Daiichi nuclear disaster in Japan in 2011 following an earthquake and tsunami.

Chernobyl stands not far from the city of Pripyat, near the border between Ukraine and Belarus. The power plant did not have any kind of containment structure, commonly used around the world, to contain the spread of radiation in case of a leak.

Most of the power generated at a nuclear power plant comes from nuclear fission, but a significant portion, about 7%, comes from the decay heat of the products used in the fission process. This decay continues for some time after a reaction is stopped, usually by an emergency SCRAM, or shutdown, of the nuclear process. Water is commonly used to cool the reactor in this event to avoid damage to the nuclear core. Reactor 4 at Chernobyl had 1,600 individual fuel channels, each one requiring 7,400 gallons (28,000 liters, 28 metric tons) of water per hour as coolant.

Cooling pumps are powered by electricity. In the event of a power grid failure, Chernobyl had three backup diesel generators. These generators could be started in 15 seconds, but took 60–75 seconds to reach full speed and produce enough electricity to power a pump.

This one-minute gap was considered an unacceptable safety risk. Within that minute, the possibility of a catastrophic nuclear event occurring was high. Chernobyl had been operating for two years without the ability to produce electricity in the first 60–75 seconds of a power loss. Nuclear engineers were trying to devise a workaround to keep electricity flowing to the coolant system, and came up with a plan to use residual momentum and steam pressure from the steam turbine to keep electricity flowing to the pumps for another 45 seconds, bridging the gap between a power failure and full power from emergency generators. Their plans just needed to be tested.

Initial tests of the plan began in 1982 and were unsuccessful. Subsequent tests in 1984 and 1985 also failed to produce the required electrical output.

In 1986, another test of the process was scheduled for April 25 during a maintenance shutdown of Reactor 4. The test would begin with an emergency shutdown of the reactor by insertion of all of the control rods. Because this had been done many times, no one believed the safety of the reactor would be compromised, so the chief reactor designer and scientific manager were not consulted; only the plant director signed off on the plan. A representative of the Soviet nuclear oversight agency, present at the plant, was not consulted either. Plant operators were eager to solve the electrical gap problem to reduce the possibility of nuclear disaster.

The test was to unfold as follows: run the reactor at a low power level, run the steam turbine up to full speed, cut the steam supply to the turbine generator, record the power output during the minute or so as the emergency generators were started, and then let the steam turbine wind down.

The plan was to be carried out during the day shift on April 25. Day shift workers were prepared ahead of time, and a team of electrical engineers was present to test the electrical output. The power output was gradually reduced starting at 1:06 a.m., so the reactor would be operating at low power by the time the day shift arrived.

While the plant was winding down for the test, another regional power station went offline unexpectedly. The electrical grid controller in Kiev asked that Chernobyl's reduction in power output be postponed, and the plant director at Chernobyl agreed. The test was put on hold.

The Kiev grid controller allowed the reactor shutdown to resume at 11:04 p.m. By that point, the day shift was long gone, the evening shift was preparing to leave, and the night shift would arrive at midnight. On the original schedule, the night shift would have only been involved in monitoring the cooling process of the already-shut down reactor.

Now the night shift had very little time to prepare to carry out a test with which they were not familiar. A rapid power reduction was initiated during the changeover from the evening to night shift. The required power output was reached at 12:05 a.m. on April 26. However, the power output continued to drop below the levels needed for the test because of a natural process known as reactor poisoning, in which short-lived fission products build up. The operator of the control rods reacted and mistakenly inserted the control rods too far, having the effect of nearly shutting down the plant completely.

With the reactor now only producing 5% of the power needed for the test, the operators, baffled by the unexpected power drop, disabled the automatic control rod system. They then manually withdrew the control rods, although standard operating procedure required that 28 of the 121 rods always be inserted to control the nuclear reaction.

Alarms were triggered repeatedly in the control room between 12:35 and 12:45. These alarms were ignored in an attempt to preserve the reactor level in order to conduct the test.

As part of the test, extra water pumps were activated to increase the water flow. As the water flowed faster through the system, it was unable to release much of its heat in the turbine and cooling towers, and the coolant temperature neared the boiling point of water, reducing the ability of plant operators to control the nuclear reaction. An alarm sounded at 1:19 indicating low steam pressure; the additional water flowing through the system was absorbing more neutrons, and causing the reactor power to drop even more. Operators responded by turning off two circulation pumps and removing more control rods to boost power output again.

By this point, the reactor configuration was terribly unstable. Nearly all of the control rods had been removed manually and the automated system to reinsert the control rods in case of emergency had been disabled. Other automated systems, such as the coolant system, had also been disabled. The reactor configuration was far outside the safety margins developed by reactor designers. If something were to cause the reactor to go supercritical, there was no way to automatically recover and prevent disaster.

Despite all this, the test continued. At 1:23:04, the steam to the turbines was shut off and the emergency generators started. Thirty-six seconds later, the emergency shutdown of the reactor was initiated. But the automated system governing the control rods was only in control of 12 rods; the rest had been manually retracted. A massive power spike caused the core to overheat; some of the control rods fractured and jammed the insertion process.

This caused the reactor to go "prompt supercritical" as power spiked at an extremely high level within seconds. Reactor output jumped to 10 times normal output. A steam explosion destroyed the reactor casing; the 2,000-ton upper plate was torn off and sent through the roof of the reactor building. The explosion severed most of the coolant lines, and the remaining coolant flashed to steam and escaped the reactor core.

Two or three seconds after the first explosion, another occurred, damaging the core and ending the nuclear chain reaction. The second explosion also destroyed more of the reactor containment vessel and ejected superheated lumps of graphite into the air, spreading radioactive fallout into outlying areas.

Chunks of burning graphite blocks rained down on the immediate area. The roof of the machine shop caught fire. Air flowed into the partially-destroyed reactor building and into the core, and the remaining graphite in the core caught fire.

The second explosion, actually a small nuclear explosion within the core, released 40 billion joules of energy, the equivalent of 10 tons of TNT.

Although prohibited by safety regulations, bitumen, which is combustible, had been used in the construction of the reactor and turbine roofs. Falling graphite, on fire, started at least five separate fires on the roof of Reactor 3, which was still operating. The night shift chief in Reactor 3, realizing it was imperative that the fires be extinguished and the cooling systems preserved, wanted to shut the reactor down immediately, but was overruled by the chief engineer. Operators in Reactor 3 were given respirators and potassium iodine tablets and told to keep working. At 5:00, the night shift chief shut down the reactor anyway, and sent away everyone except the operators needed to operate the emergency cooling system.

Radiation levels in some areas of the damaged plant gave unprotected workers lethal doses in less than a minute. However, the dosimeters inside the plant were either damaged or not working, and crew chiefs could not ascertain the actual radiation level. The reactor crew chief came to the conclusion that the reactor was intact, ignoring the fact that burning pieces of graphite and reactor fuel were scattered around the building and fires had broken out. The crew chief stayed with his crew until morning as they pumped water into the reactor. None wore protective gear, and most were dead from radiation exposure within weeks.

Shortly after the explosions, firefighters arrived, including the Chernobyl Power Station firefighters, who were not aware that the fires were anything more than electrical. No one told them about the radioactive smoke and debris, and most also died within weeks.

The fires on the roof and around the buildings were extinguished by 5:00 p.m.. Helicopters dropped more than 5,500 tons (5,000 metric tons) of sand, lead, clay, and boron onto the burning reactor. One of the helicopters collided with a cable on a construction crane; the helicopter crashed near the reactor, killing the four-man crew. Practically none of the neutron-absorbing materials reached the core. The fire inside the core of Reactor 4 continued to burn until May 10.

The firefighters, suffering from radiation poisoning, reported a metallic taste in their mouth and the feeling of pins and needles in their face.

Residents around the reactors watched as a radioactive cloud rose from the plant. The explosion and raging fire had thrown radioactive isotopes such as cesium-137, iodine-131, and strontium-90 into the air.

Remote-controlled bulldozers and robot-like vehicles were brought in to detect radioactivity and move hot debris. But in the high radiation field, the electronics failed.

The residents of the nearby town of Pripyat went on with their day, oblivious to the events at the power plant. Within a few hours, dozens of residents became ill, with a metallic taste in their mouths, severe headaches, coughing, and vomiting.

The plant was controlled by Soviet authorities, who did not disseminate information to the local population. Later in the morning, information started coming out that there had been a fire at the power plant, but it had been put out and everything was fine.

A commission was convened the same day to determine what had happened. By the time they arrived at the power plant that evening, two people had already died and 52 were in the hospital. Soon they had evidence that the reactor had been destroyed, and high levels of radiation had escaped, exposing people in the area. In the early morning hours of April 27, more than 24 hours after the explosion, they ordered the evacuation of Pripyat.

The people of Pripyat were told they would be evacuated for three days. Buses arrived at 11:00 a.m., and the evacuation began at 2:00 p.m. By 3:00 p.m., 53,000 people had been evacuated. The following day, the evacuation zone was increased to 6.2 miles (10 km). Ten days later the exclusion zone was expanded to 19 miles (30 km). This exclusion zone has basically remained in place ever since. Local residents have never been allowed to return.

The initial evacuations had taken place with no public announcements from the Soviets about the reason. On April 28, radiation levels on workers' clothing set off alarms at the Forsmark Nuclear Power Plant in Sweden, about 680 miles (1,100 km) from Chernobyl. Investigators sought an explanation for the radiation, and, determining that it was not from their power plant, announced that a radioactive cloud was spreading over Europe, most likely the result of some event in the western Soviet Union.

So, in the evening two days after the event, an announcer on the Soviet TV news program *Vremya* read a 20-second statement saying that there had been an accident at Chernobyl, and its effects were being dealt with. TASS, the state-owned news agency, then went on to talk about Three Mile Island and other American nuclear accidents, an oft-used Soviet tactic of emphasizing foreign disasters when one had occurred in the Soviet Union. The announcement of a commission to study the event, and subsequent state radio broadcasts of classical music, alerted Soviet citizens to the fact that a tragedy had occurred.

About the same time, American news outlets started reporting on the disaster.

Meanwhile, the burning reactor core at Reactor 4 was still causing problems. Water accumulating from ruptured coolant lines and the firefighting operation was creating a serious risk of a steam explosion. The burning reactor fuel and graphite, at temperatures higher than 2,200°F (1,200°C), started to burn through the reactor floor and mix with molten concrete to create corium, a radioactive semi-liquid similar to lava. If this material melted through the floor into the pool of accumulated water below it, a serious steam explosion would eject more radioactive material into the air. Three equipment operators donned diving suits and entered the pool of water to open valves to drain the water pool. They received lethal doses of radiation while in the water.

By May 8, the task was complete, with 22,000 tons (20,000 metric tons) of highly radioactive water removed. With the water pool gone, the radioactive mass would have to melt through the ground all the way to the water table to create a steam explosion. To reduce that likelihood, liquid nitrogen was injected beneath the reactor to freeze the earth. Injection began on May 4, but scientists soon determined that 27 tons (25 metric tons) of liquid nitrogen per day was required to keep the ground frozen at -148°F (-100°C). The idea was scrapped and the room under the reactor where the cooling system had been was filled with concrete.

Government officials rounded up liquidators, "volunteer" workers from the surrounding areas, to assist with the cleanup of the reactor site. They collected the worst of the radioactive debris and shoveled it into what was left of the reactor, wearing heavy protective gear. These workers were called "bio-robots" by the military. The presence of the radioactive graphite blocks and other debris limited the time the liquidators could spend in the immediate area to 40 seconds at a time.

Nuclear engineers still feared that the remains of the reactor could yet begin a self-sustaining nuclear reaction and cause another explosion. To prevent this, officials devised a new containment structure to prevent rain from triggering another event. By December, in the largest civil engineering task in history, a concrete sarcophagus had been erected over the reactor, sealing it and its contents. At least 250,000 workers received a special "clean-up medal," as well as a maximum lifetime radiation dosage.

Liquidators were given little information about the hazards of the job they had been recruited to do. Most of them exceeded safe radiation limits, some by as much as 100 times. Many quickly died.

The vehicles used by the clean-up crews, including cars, trucks, planes, and helicopters, remain to this day parked nearby in a field referred to as the vehicle graveyard.

Chernobyl Nuclear Power Plant in 2011 with its sarcophagus in place.

While the sarcophagus was being constructed, a scientific team entered the reactor to see if there was further risk of explosion. They recorded high temperatures near the core. They discovered a highly-radioactive mass in the basement, more than 6 feet (2 m) wide and weighing hundreds of tons. It was made of sand and glass, as well as nuclear fuel from the reactor. The concrete below it was steaming hot, and had been penetrated by the solidified nuclear lava, creating never-before-seen crystalline forms subsequently named chernobylite. The expedition exposed the participants to high levels of radiation, but they came to the conclusion that the risk of explosion had been eliminated.

The Soviet government embarked on a massive clean-up effort. The official reason was to repopulate the area and re-cultivate the fields. Within 15 months, 75% of the land was brought back into cultivation, although only a third of the evacuated villages were resettled.

Investigations into the cause of the disaster focused on both operator error and plant design deficiencies. The safety systems in place, as well as their implementation, were also questioned. Investigators likened the test to airplane pilots experimenting with their engines in flight. Reports blamed a deficient safety culture at the Chernobyl plant as well as throughout the Soviet Union in general, especially in the design, operation, and regulation of the nuclear industry.

The physical effect of the disaster on a wide area was substantial. The accident released 400 times more radioactive material than the nuclear bombing of Hiroshima. Worst hit was a wide swath of Belarus, Ukraine, and Russia, where 38,000 square miles (100,000 square kilometers) were significantly contaminated; this is an area larger than the state of Indiana and nearly as large as Switzerland. Lower levels of radiation were measured over all of Europe with the exception of Spain and Portugal.

The level of contamination in Europe varied by location. Mountainous areas, such as the Alps, Scottish Highlands, and Welsh mountains were more heavily contaminated; clouds cooled as they climbed over the highlands and dropped contaminated rain. A cold front moving across Sweden and Norway at the time of the radiological release brought rain and therefore heavy contamination to those countries.

As radioactive contamination spread toward more populous areas of the Soviet Union, the Soviet air force seeded clouds over Belorussian SSR, forcing the contaminated rain to fall. Gomel, the second largest city in Belorussian SSR, reported a heavy, black-colored rainfall. About 60% of the contamination fell on that Soviet republic.

The Pripyat River flows past Chernobyl and drains into the Dnieper River, forming one of the largest surface water systems in Europe. The river supplied water to the 2.4 million residents of Kiev, the capital of Ukraine some 65 miles (105 km) from Chernobyl. The river was in full spring flood mode when it became contaminated with radioactive particles, causing concern for the safety of the drinking water. Soviet guidelines for ingesting radioiodine were temporarily raised so that the government could report most water as safe, and even a year later reported the plant's cooling ponds as safe. The Soviet government also told citizens that all the contaminants in the Dnieper River had settled to the bottom in an insoluble state and would not dissolve for 800–1,000 years. Despite these reassurances, the Kiev water supply was switched to the Desna River two months after the nuclear event, and around the plant massive silt traps and an underground barrier were built to prevent contaminated groundwater from leaking into the

Pripyat River.

Following the disaster, the pine forest downwind of the reactor turned reddish-brown and died. Most domestic animals were removed from the exclusion zone, but many of the wild animals died or stopped reproducing. Horses left on a nearby island died because their thyroid glands were destroyed by radiation; cattle on the same island died or suffered from thyroid damage as well. The next generations appeared to be normal, though.

Ukrainian farms reported that in the first four years after the disaster, almost 350 animals with gross deformities were born, whereas, in the five years before the radiological release, only three abnormal births took place. These deformities included extra limbs; missing limbs; missing ribs, eyes, or heads; and deformed skulls. Despite this, the World Health Organization states that there was no statistical difference before or after the disaster for human deformities.

Effects of the contamination continued for years. In 2010, wild boars in Germany were still found to be contaminated by radiation from Chernobyl. In 2009, Norwegians were still providing uncontaminated feed for livestock to ensure that radiation levels in slaughtered animals remained below acceptable levels of contamination. The United Kingdom had to restrict contaminated sheep from entering the human food chain; the restrictions were not fully lifted until 2012.

A robot has more recently been sent into the destroyed reactor, and has brought back samples of black radiotrophic fungi growing on the reactor walls.

It is difficult to determine the human toll, partly because of Soviet secrecy and misinformation, and partly because it is impossible to track the exact origin of cancers that appear later. The explosion and fires resulted in 237 people suffering from acute radiation sickness; 31 of them died within three months. Most of them were fire and rescue workers who responded to the explosion and had no idea how dangerous the situation was.

In 2005, the Chernobyl Forum, composed of the International Atomic Energy Agency, other UN agencies, and the governments of Russia, Ukraine, and Belarus, released a report on the environmental and health consequences of the accident. The report states that 28 emergency responders died from acute radiation poisoning and 15 patients died from thyroid cancer. It estimated that about 4,000 of the 5 million residents of the contaminated areas could be expected to die from cancer within 80 years of the event.

Belarus reports that only 150 of the 66,000 emergency responders and liquidators died in the first decade after the accident. Congenital defects in the country rose by 40% within six years and became the principal cause of infant mortality. There was a substantial increase in disease and cancers, and in one highly contaminated area, 95% of the children in 2005 had at least one chronic illness. Nearly a quarter of Belarus was contaminated.

Ukraine says that 5,722 cleanup workers died through 1995. In 1993, the Ukrainian Ministry of Health claimed that 70% of its population was unwell, with a large increase in chronic illnesses. By the year 2000, 3.5 million Ukrainian citizens (5% of the population) were receiving benefits for suffering from radiation; many of these people were current or former workers at the Chernobyl plant, or had been resettled from the exclusion zones.

Approximately 600,000 liquidators were engaged in the plant cleanup; half of them were "bio-robots," working in such extreme radiological conditions that electronic robots ceased to function. Most of them suffered from premature aging and many have died; cancer rates are substantially higher than the general population. Greenpeace claims that by 2000, 200,000 people had died from the accident.

The Soviet government systematically covered up the extent of the damage to the population's health. Most cases of acute radiation sickness were reclassified as Vegetovascular dystonia (VvD), a Soviet classification for a type of panic disorder with symptoms similar to acute radiation sickness. Declassified documents show that the Soviet Health Ministry ordered the reclassification of those who did not show signs of burns or hair loss, and for all liquidators who had exceeded their maximum allowed dose. The Soviets referred to VvD as "radiophobia."

The 2005 Chernobyl Forum report states that one of the main health impacts has been thyroid cancer in children. Of 4,000 cases reported, there were nine deaths. Other studies indicate the number of Chernobyl-caused thyroid cancers in children could be as high as 6,000 before 2005.

Mental health of the survivors continues to be a problem. Many of the adolescents and young adults near the contamination zones are unsure of the actual effects and consider themselves fatally flawed; illicit drug use and unprotected sex is rampant because of a sense of victimization and hopelessness. Requests for abortions out of fear of radiation poisoning and its effects on the fetus have also been higher since the accident all over Europe, as people who were children when the contamination occurred are now of childbearing age.

The economic cost of the disaster has been massive. Mikhail Gorbachev claims the Soviet Union spent US$18 billion on containment and decontamination, nearly bankrupting the government. The total cost over the last 30 years in Belarus is estimated to be US$235 billion, with Chernobyl-related spending falling from 22% of the national budget in 1991 to 6% in 2002. Between 5% and 7% of government spending in Ukraine continues to be related to Chernobyl. Most of the ongoing costs are social benefits being paid to about 7,000,000 people in Belarus, Ukraine, and Russia.

The removal of 1,938,100 acres (784,320 ha) of agricultural land and 1,715,000 acres (694,200 ha) of forest land from production impacted the area significantly. However, special cultivation techniques, fertilizers, and other additives have brought much of that land back into production since.

When Ukraine and Belarus became independent in 1991, they lowered the legal radiation threshold and therefore expanded the contamination zones. More than 500,000 people have been resettled; many of them are now welfare recipients. Ukraine continues to maintain the reactor complex, employing a massive workforce to keep any individual's exposure to a minimum. All construction work on the unfinished Reactors 5 and 6 at Chernobyl were permanently halted three years after the disaster. The damaged Reactor 4 was sealed off with the sarcophagus, but Reactors 1 through 3 continued to operate because of an energy shortage in Ukraine.

In 1991, a fire in the turbine building damaged Reactor 2 beyond repair and it was taken offline. Reactor 1 was decommissioned in 1996, and Reactor 3 was shut down in 2000, ending nuclear power generation at Chernobyl.

Because the 24-story sarcophagus was designed and constructed quickly with only a 30-year life span, a new containment system needed to be in place by 2016. The Chernobyl New Safe Confinement was to be in place by

2005, but the project suffered from ongoing delays; the completion date has been moved to 2017, although many suspect it won't be finished until 2020. This immense structure, designed to cover both the damaged reactor and the sarcophagus, is a metal arch 303 feet (92 m) high with a span of 886 feet (270 m) by 804 feet (245 m). It is being constructed adjacent to the reactor and will be slid into place on rails. The Chernobyl Shelter Fund is paying for the cost of the structure, estimated to be $2.2 billion, with help from international donors. It is the largest moveable structure ever built.

The new massive steel covering being constructed to replace the sarcophagus and entomb Reactor 4.

A section of the turbine building roof collapsed on February 12, 2013 due to inadequate maintenance and repairs of the aging structure. The former deputy director of the plant warned that the complex was on the verge of collapse. Radioactivity levels increased again around the plant, and 225 workers employed at the plant or at the construction of the new shelter were evacuated for a short time. The sarcophagus structure is now leaky and structurally unsound. Scientists fear that its collapse could stir up enough radioactivity to cause another disaster, even worse than the original event.

Plans continue to be developed for disposal of the remaining nuclear fuel and contamination at the complex, as Ukraine would like to completely clear the site. Workers can only work one 15-minute shift inside the sarcophagus each day due to high radioactivity levels.

Approximately 95% of the fuel from Reactor 4, weighing 200 tons (180 metric tons), is still inside the remains of the reactor building; it consists of core fragments, dust, and lava-like material that hardened into a ceramic form. When, how, or if this lava will dissolve or break down and release its radiation is unclear.

The fenced-in 19-mile (30-km) exclusion zone, called the "zone of alienation," continues today. It is uninhabited except for about 300 people who refuse to leave. The area has largely reverted to forestland, which, if it catches fire, will spread the radioactive contamination yet again. Ukrainian officials say the area will not be fit for human habitation for another 20,000 years.

Ukraine opened the exclusion zone to Chernobyl tourists in 2011.

The political repercussions are immense, too. The people of Italy and the government of Germany have decided to end the use of nuclear power. The accident at Chernobyl and the world's reaction to Soviet secrecy, especially by Soviet citizens themselves, gave rise to the new Soviet policy of glasnost (open discussion, transparency, and dissemination of information) and perestroika (restructuring of the Soviet government and society). Glasnost and perestroika, in short order, paved the way for the downfall of the Soviet empire and the dissolution of the U.S.S.R. in December 1991.

50

Great Kantō Earthquake

1923

Japan

"Yokohama, the city of almost half a million souls, had become a vast plain of fire, of red, devouring sheets of flame which played and flickered. Here and there a remnant of a building, a few shattered walls, stood up like rocks above the expanse of flame, unrecognizable... It was as if the very earth were now burning. It presented exactly the aspect of a gigantic Christmas pudding over which the spirits were blazing, devouring nothing. For the city was gone." —Henry W. Kinney, Tokyo-based editor for *Trans-Pacific* magazine

Along the northwestern Pacific Ring of Fire, the Philippine Sea tectonic plate continually undergoes subduction beneath the Okhotsk Plate; the resulting fault line follows the Sagami Trough along the southern coastline of Japan. At 11:58 a.m. on Saturday, September 1, 1923, this earthquake fault ruptured. The resultant earthquake was the Great Kantō Earthquake, with a magnitude of 7.9. It was focused deep underground beneath Izu Ōshima Island in Sagami Bay.

The quake, or actually a series of quakes, shook the Kantō Plain on the island of Honshu for between four and ten minutes. Tokyo, home to more than 2,250,000 people, and the booming international port city of Yokohama were devastated.

The earthquake struck at lunchtime, while many people were cooking their noon meal over open fires. Large fires broke out and swept across both cities, the fire fueled by collapsed wooden houses. As people fled burning neighborhoods, their feet became stuck in the melting tarmac, and many died. People jumped into the Sumida River from crowded riverbanks or burning bridges in order to escape the flames, and many drowned. Bridges collapsed from the weight of all the people trying to cross them at the same time. Many others burned to death in streets, alleyways, and open spaces as they tried to flee the flames.

A typhoon was battering northern Japan at the time, and higher winds in the Tokyo-Yokohama area helped fan the fires. Some of the raging fires merged and developed into five distinct firestorms. Winds were funneled down narrow streets, and vortices of wind and flame formed at intersections, creating fire tornados, or firenadoes. A large number of people sought refuge in the Honjo Army Clothing Depot in downtown Tokyo, one of the few large open spaces. A 300-foot (91-m) high firenado formed and struck the depot, incinerating all but 300 of the 44,000 people taking cover there.

As is often the case in major quakes, water mains broke, hampering the firefighting effort. It was two days before the raging fires were extinguished; about 6,400 people died in the fires, which destroyed about 381,000 homes.

The heavy rainfall from the typhoon, as well as earthquake damage, caused landslides in the mountains and hills in Kanagawa Prefecture; 800 were killed. One of the landslides swept the entire village of Nebukawa, along with 100 passengers traveling on a train, into the sea.

Within minutes of the quake, a tsunami, as much as 39.5 feet (12 m) high, struck the coast, killing even more. One hundred people on a beach in Kamakura and 50 people on a causeway in Enoshima were swept away. More than 570,000 homes were destroyed by the tsunami, and 1.9 million were left homeless.

The battlecruiser *Amagi*, in drydock undergoing conversion to an aircraft carrier, was damaged beyond repair and had to be scrapped. Unusual swells and currents in the Pacific, caused by the earthquake, led to the Honda Point disaster near Santa Barbara, California, when seven American destroyers went aground on September 8 and sank, killing 27, in the largest peacetime loss of naval ships in U.S. history.

The Great Kantō Earthquake was the worst natural disaster in pre-war Japanese history. The death toll has been estimated to be 142,800, and includes about 40,000 people who went missing and were never found. Forty-eight percent of Tokyo's homes were totally destroyed or rendered uninhabitable, leaving nearly 1.4 million people homeless. Yokohama had another 781,000 people left homeless. Most of the region's hospitals, schools, factories, and banks were destroyed, leaving the populace destitute. Damage was estimated at US$1 billion, more than $14 billion today. The economic cost was roughly four times the nation's annual budget in 1923. Nearly half of the city of Tokyo was reduced to rubble. Thousands of aftershocks continued over the course of the next few days.

A view of the destruction in Yokohama.

The Japanese Home Ministry declared martial law to enforce order and security. Rumors spread that Koreans were taking advantage of the disaster by planting bombs and committing arson and robbery. Japan had occupied

Korea since 1905, and ruled it with an iron grip. The post-quake rumors (which were false) helped stoke anti-Korean sentiment; mobs in Tokyo and Yokohama killed 231 Koreans during the first week of September. Independent reports disputed that number, provided by the Japanese government, and said the death toll from anti-Korean mobs was more like 6,000 to 10,000.

Some newspapers reported the anti-Korean rumors as fact and said that the Koreans were setting fires and poisoning wells. The spreading flames and the presence of cloudy drinking water (in reality an effect of the quake) seemed to prove the allegations for the survivors. Vigilante groups (called "Self-Defense Committees"), sometimes aided by the military, set up roadblocks and tested people for a Korean accent. Those who failed the test were deported, beaten, or killed. Some of these victims turned out to be Chinese, Okinawans, or Japanese citizens speaking with a regional dialect. Some 700 Chinese citizens were among the dead.

When Koreans were found, witnesses reported they were beaten to death with clubs or crowbars, hacked to pieces with swords, or pierced with spears. One was tied to a pole, and every passing native beat him in retribution.

The earthquake and then the massacres began making headlines around the world. Sensitive to the world's opinion, the government began to censor news reports. They were especially concerned with what might happen if word of the atrocities spread to Korea, then under Japanese control. Travel from Japan to Korea was curtailed to prevent word of the atrocities from spreading there and possibly fomenting a rebellion. While Japan controlled the newspapers printed in Korea, they could not control the spread of information by foreign newspapers, some of which made their way to Korea. Japan finally conceded that some innocent Korean blood had been spilled while dealing with Koreans guilty of arson, looting, and violence.

The government responded by calling upon the Japanese Army to protect Koreans. The army passed out flyers denying the rumors and warning of the consequences of attacks against Koreans, but the warnings did little good. The army placed 23,715 Koreans in protective custody across Japan; 12,000 of them were in Tokyo. Some 750 Koreans were placed on a boat in Yokohama Harbor for their safety; the water, covered in an oil slick from tanks burst during the earthquake and tsunami, caught fire and the Koreans burned to death.

While mob violence continued, the regional police and the Imperial Army used the chaos to eliminate some of the political dissidents in the country. They targeted socialists, anarchists, and communists for abduction and death, claiming that dissidents were using the crisis to try to overthrow the Japanese government.

The government mobilized troops from all over Japan and sent them to Tokyo and Yokohama to assist in relief and recovery efforts, as well as repair damaged infrastructure. Eventually, one in five members of the nation's army was deployed to the disaster zone.

During the first week of the recovery effort, the Navy repaired damaged docks and rebuilt piers in order to accommodate relief shipments. The army had to rebuild 53 miles (85 km) of rail track and build 27 temporary bridges across the rivers in Tokyo so that relief supplies could be distributed. City officials initiated the construction of temporary barracks in the city's parks to house the homeless. More than half a million survivors returned to the site of their homes and constructed makeshift shelters.

The first task was to remove the dead from the streets, waterways, and open spaces of the city. Fifteen collection centers opened, and 300 city employees collected bodies with motorized carts, pushcarts, and horse-drawn wagons. By September 11, 47,200 bodies had been collected, and another 10,525 were removed from the city's waterways. Thousands of bodies were taken to mass crematoriums; the haze from burning bodies hung over the city for weeks.

Other countries sent aid to Japan; about 70% of the international aid came from the U.S. About $20 million worth of cash and supplies were donated by American agencies and citizens, about 2.4% of the gross domestic product of the U.S. at the time. It was the first modern international relief effort, partially spurred on by the advent of modern communications. Within a week, dozens of American warships were in port to distribute relief supplies. Japanese authorities, intent on proving they could handle the situation without interference from the West, supposedly jammed radio communications on the relief ships and tried to prevent them from docking. Relations between Japan and the U.S. suffered.

Initially, the Japanese interpreted the disaster as an act of divine punishment for their self-centeredness and immorality. Later, the feeling emerged that Japan had been given a chance to rebuild their cities as well as their culture and values. Right-wing forces in the country emerged from the disaster in a stronger position; before the quake, Japan was moving closer to the West and a more democratic government, but in the coming years Japan would become more militaristic as World War II approached.

For a time, the Japanese considered rebuilding their capital elsewhere. In the end, Tokyo was rebuilt with a modern road and railroad network. Many parks were established to provide places of refuge. The site of the firenado is now Yokoamicho Park, home to the main memorial to the earthquake victims; it holds the ashes of 58,000 victims.

September 1 is Disaster Prevention Day in Japan, in commemoration of the Great Kantō Earthquake. Schools and other organizations hold disaster drills. A moment of silence is held in schools at 11:58 out of respect for those who were killed. Today, disaster-preparedness programs in Japan stress the importance of using portable radios to obtain reliable information in the case of disaster, and not to be misled by rumors.

Bibliography

1. Great Molasses Flood

http://en.wikipedia.org/wiki/Boston_Molasses_Disaster

http://www.theamericanstoryteller.com/?ms_song=molasses

Bridgeport Standard Telegram, Connecticut, 1919-01-16.

Park, Edwards, "Eric Postpischil's Molasses Disaster Pages, Smithsonian Article". Retrieved from http://edp.org/molpark.htm, 1 March 2015.

Jabr, Ferris (July 17, 2013). "The Science of the Great Molasses Flood". *Scientific American*. Retrieved from http://www.scientificamerican.com/article/molasses-flood-physics-science/

Mason, John, "Eric Postpischil's Molasses Disaster Pages, Yankee Magazine Article". Retrieved from http://edp.org/molyank.htm

Schworm, Peter (January 15, 2015). "Nearly a century later, new insight into cause of Great Molasses Flood of 1919". *Boston Globe*.

Puleo, Stephen (2004). "Dark Tide: The Great Boston Molasses Flood of 1919". Boston: Beacon Press.

2. Lac-Mégantic Rail Disaster

http://en.wikipedia.org/wiki/Lac-M%C3%A9gantic_rail_disaster

Summary of the Transportation Safety Board of Canada's (TSB) Railway Investigation Report R13D0054. Retrieved from http://www.tsb.gc.ca/eng/rapports-reports/rail/2013/r13d0054/r13d0054-r-es.asp

Railway Investigation Report (long version of the TSB report). Retrieved from http://www.tsb.gc.ca/eng/rapports-reports/rail/2013/r13d0054/r13d0054.asp

TSBCanada animation at

https://www.youtube.com/watch?v=wVMNspPc8Zc

Audio and text of conversations between the locomotive engineer and rail traffic controllers both before and after the derailment, retrieved from http://www.theglobeandmail.com/news/national/dispatches-from-a-disaster/article20148699/#dashboard/follows/

3. Iroquois Theatre Fire

https://en.wikipedia.org/wiki/Iroquois_Theatre_fire

"The Iroquois Theater Fire". Eastland Memorial Society. Retrieved from http://www.eastlandmemorial.org/iroquois.shtml

"Fire Inquiry Discloses: Skylights Reported Opened After the Disaster—Cannot Find the 'Asbestos' Curtain—Usher Arrested". *The New York Times,* 5 January 1904. Retrieved from http://query.nytimes.com/mem/archive-free/pdf?res=9A06E1DC1E3AE733A25756C0A9679C946597D6CF

Actor Eddie Foy's personal account, "A Tragedy Remembered". *NPFA Journal* (National Fire Protection Association), July/August. 1995. Retrieved from http://nfpatoday.blog.nfpa.org/2011/12/today-in-fire-history-iroquois-theatre-fire.html

Verdict of Coroner's Jury at http://wiki.genealogytoday.com/Chicago_Theater_Disaster_1903_Verdict_of_Coroner's_Jury.html

"This Day In History: Fire Breaks Out In Chicago Theater". The History Channel. Retrieved from http://www.history.com/this-day-in-history/fire-breaks-out-in-chicago-theater

Zasky, Jason. "Burning Down the House: The 1903 Iroquois Theater Fire". *Failure Magazine.* Retrieved from http://failuremag.com/feature/article/burning_down_the_house/

4. Al-Aaimmah Bridge Stampede

http://en.wikipedia.org/wiki/2005_Al-Aaimmah_bridge_stampede

https://en.wikipedia.org/wiki/Al-Aimmah_Bridge

"Iran blames disaster on 'suspicious hands'". Theage.com.au. 2005-09-01.

http://news.bbc.co.uk/2/hi/middle_east/4199618.stm

http://www.theguardian.com/world/2005/sep/01/iraq.rorycarroll1

http://www.cnn.com/2005/WORLD/meast/09/01/iraq.main/index.html

5. Cavalese Cable Car Disaster

http://en.wikipedia.org/wiki/Cavalese_cable_car_disaster_%281998%29

Tagliabue, John with Wald, Matthew L., "Death in the Alps: a Special Report; How Wayward U.S. Pilot Killed 20 on Ski Lift". *The New York Times*, 18 February 1998.

Dejevsky, Mary (5 March 1999). "Cable car pilot not guilty of killings". *The Independent*.

"Italian outrage over cable car tragedy". BBC news, 4 February 1998.

"Jury Sentences Marine in Ski-Lift Incident to Dismissal". *New York Times*, 3 April 1999.

"Investigators Blame Marines for Cable Car Accident". American Forces Press Service. 16 Mar 1998.

Rizzo, Alessandra (Feb 8, 1998). "Italian Government Calls American Pilots Criminal". Rome, Italy: ABCNews.

6. SL-1 Meltdown

http://en.wikipedia.org/wiki/SL-1

http://www.radiationworks.com/sl1reactor.htm

Stratton, William R. *LA-3611. A Review of Criticality Accidents*, Los Alamos Scientific Laboratory, 1967.

Maslin, Janet (March 21, 1984). "Sl-1 (1983): Looking at Perils of Toxicity". *The New York Times*.

7. Basra Mass Grain Poisoning

http://en.wikipedia.org/wiki/1971_Iraq_poison_grain_disaster

Skerfving SB, Copplestone JF (1976). "Poisoning caused by the consumption of organomercury-dressed seed in Iraq". *Bull. World Health Organ.* 1976; 54(1): 101–112.

http://www.ncbi.nlm.nih.gov/pmc/articles/PMC2366450/pdf/bullw ho00452-0108.pdf

8. Centralia Underground Fire

http://en.wikipedia.org/wiki/Centralia_mine_fire

Currie, Tyler (April 2, 2003), "Zip Code 00000". *Washington Post.*

Holmes, Kristin E. (October 21, 2008). "Minding a legacy of faith: In an empty town, a shrine still shines". Philly.com.

DeKok, David (2010). "Fire Underground: The Ongoing Tragedy of the Centralia Mine Fire." Globe Pequot Press.

O'Carroll, Eoin (February 5, 2010). "Centralia, Pa.: How an underground coal fire erased a town". *Bright Green blog*. The Christian Science Monitor.

Krajick, Kevin (May 2005), "Fire in the hole", *Smithsonian Magazine.*

9. *Sultana* Steamboat Explosion

http://en.wikipedia.org/wiki/SS_Sultana

Rule, G.E.; Rule, Deb (December 2001). "The Sultana: A case for sabotage". *North and South Magazine* 5 (1).

Berry, Chester D. (2005) [1892]. "Loss of the Sultana and Reminiscences of Survivors". University of Tennessee Press.

Huffman, Alan (October 2009). "Surviving the Worst: The Wreck of the Sultana at the End of the American Civil War". *Mississippi Historical Society.*

http://www.unexplainedfiles.com/2009/10/sultana-titanic-of-mississippi.html

http://thisweekinthecivilwar.com/?p=311/

10. Door to Hell Fire

http://en.wikipedia.org/wiki/Door_to_Hell

"Turkmenistan hopes 'Door to Hell' will boost tourism". CTV News, 22 June 2014. Retreived from http://www.ctvnews.ca/sci-tech/turkmenistan-hopes-door-to-hell-will-boost-tourism-1.1880647

Nunez, Christina (16 July 2014). "Q&A: The First-Ever Expedition to Turkmenistan's 'Door to Hell'". *National Geographic.* Retrieved from http://news.nationalgeographic.com/news/energy/2014/07/140716-door-to-hell-darvaza-crater-george-kourounis-expedition/

http://rt.com/news/167548-hellish-attractive-gas-crater/

11. Triangle Shirtwaist Factory Fire

http://en.wikipedia.org/wiki/Triangle_Shirtwaist_Factory_fire

"Triangle Shirtwaist Factory Building", National Park Service. Retrieved from http://www.nps.gov/nr/travel/pwwmh/ny30.htm

http://failuremag.com/feature/article/the_triangle_shirtwaist_fire/

McFarlane, Arthur E. "Fire and the Skyscraper: The Problem of Protecting the Workers in New York's Tower Factories." McClure Magazine, Vol. XXXVII, No. 5, September, 1911. Retrieved from http://books.google.com/books?id=IBZykg_-9IAC&pg=PA466-IA2&#v=onepage&q&f=false

12. Sampoong Department Store Collapse

http://en.wikipedia.org/wiki/Sampoong_Department_Store_collapse

"The Dawn of Modern Korea — Collapse of Sampoong Department Store", *The Korea Times*. Retrieved from http://web.archive.org/web/20070314002032/http://times.hankooki.com/lpage/opinion/200410/kt2004101418510554130.htm

"Korean store owner, son sentenced for role in collapse". CNN. 27 December 1995. Retrieved from http://edition.cnn.com/WORLD/9512/skorea_store/sentencing/index.html

13. Collinwood School Fire

http://en.wikipedia.org/wiki/Collinwood_school_fire

"Hunt for Guilty in Ohio Holocaust". *Chicago Tribune,* March 5, 1908. p. 1. Retrieved from http://archives.chicagotribune.com/1908/03/05/page/1/article/hunt-for-guilty-in-ohio-holocaust

Dissell, Rachel. "Collinwood school fire: 100 years later, an angel still kneels over the children". *The Plain Dealer.*

Jablonski, Ray (2001). "Tragic past leads to present lessons". *Sun Newspapers*. Retrieved from http://ech.case.edu/ech-cgi/article.pl?id=CSF

http://web.archive.org/web/20020907113155/http://www.sunnews.com/news/2001/part2/1018/ETRAGIC.htm

14. *Aleksandr Suvorov* Cruise Ship Disaster

http://en.wikipedia.org/wiki/Aleksandr_Suvorov_%28ship%29

http://www.ship-technology.com/features/featurethe-worlds-deadliest-cruise-ship-disasters-4181089/

https://news.google.com/newspapers?nid=1298&dat=19830608&id=YwJOAAAAIBAJ&sjid=GIwDAAAAIBAJ&pg=6345,3568692&hl=en

15. Bhola Cyclone

http://www.hurricanescience.org/history/storms/1970s/greatbhola/

http://en.wikipedia.org/wiki/1970_Bhola_cyclone

http://en.wikipedia.org/wiki/Indian_independence_movement

http://en.wikipedia.org/wiki/East_Pakistan

http://en.wikipedia.org/wiki/Dominion_of_Pakistan

http://en.wikipedia.org/wiki/Indo-Pakistani_War_of_1971

http://en.wikipedia.org/wiki/Bangladesh

http://en.wikipedia.org/wiki/Bangladesh_Awami_League

http://en.wikipedia.org/wiki/Bangladesh_Liberation_War

http://en.wikipedia.org/wiki/1971_Bangladesh_genocide

http://en.wikipedia.org/wiki/Pakistan_and_weapons_of_mass_destruction

http://www.weather.com/storms/hurricane/news/deadliest-cyclone-history-bangladesh-20130605#/1

https://geol105naturalhazards.voices.wooster.edu/the-great-bhola-cyclone/

Frank, Neil; Husain, S. A. (June 1971). "The deadliest tropical cyclone in history?". *Bulletin of the American Meteorological Society.* American Meteorological Society. Retrieved from http://journals.ametsoc.org/doi/pdf/10.1175/1520-0477%281971%29052%3C0438%3ATDTCIH%3E2.0.CO%3B2

16. Halifax Explosion

https://en.wikipedia.org/wiki/Halifax_Explosion

Gilligan, Edmund (February 1938). "Death in Halifax". *American Mercury* 43 (170): 175–181. Retrieved from http://www.unz.org/Pub/AmMercury-1938feb-00175?View=PDF&apages=0057

https://en.wikipedia.org/wiki/SS_Imo

https://en.wikipedia.org/wiki/SS_Mont-Blanc

CBC Halifax Explosion Retrieved from http://www.cbc.ca/halifaxexplosion/

A Vision of Regeneration, Nova Scotia Archives. Retrieved from http://novascotia.ca/archives/virtual/explosion/

17. Big Bayou Canot Train Wreck

http://en.wikipedia.org/wiki/1993_Big_Bayou_Canot_train_wreck

Holloway, David. "*Mobile Press-Register* 200th Anniversary: Sunset Limited train wreck memories not diminished by passing years", 1 July 2013.

U.S. National Transportation Safety Board Railroad-Marine Accident Report 94-1, 19 September 1994.

Labaton, Stephen (June 22, 1994). "Barge Pilot Blamed in Fatal Amtrak Wreck". *The New York Times*.

"No Criminal Liability Is Found in Amtrak Bayou Derailment". *Los Angeles Times*. March 26, 1994.

Sproul, R. C. "Train Wreck Eyewitness account of aftermath". Ligonier Ministries blog.

18. The Beer and Pretzel Stampede at Khodynka

http://en.wikipedia.org/wiki/Khodynka_Tragedy

http://en.wikipedia.org/wiki/Revolution_of_1905

http://en.wikipedia.org/wiki/Russian_Revolution

http://worldhistoryproject.org/1896/5/18/khodynka-tragedy

http://www.rus-sky.com/history/library/diaris/1896.htm

http://en.wikipedia.org/wiki/Khodynka_Field

Memories of Alexei Volkov retrieved from
http://www.alexanderpalace.org/volkov/4.html

http://lisawallerrogers.com/2011/06/27/nicholas-alexandra-khodynka-field/

19. European Heatwave

http://en.wikipedia.org/wiki/2003_European_heat_wave

http://en.wikipedia.org/wiki/1995_Chicago_heat_wave

http://en.wikipedia.org/wiki/Summer_2012_North_American_heat_wave

"WMO: Unprecedented sequence of extreme weather events".
Retrieved from
http://www.preventionweb.net/english/professional/news/v.php?id=14970

"French heat toll almost 15,000". BBC News. Retrieved from
http://news.bbc.co.uk/2/hi/europe/3139694.stm

"French death report points finger". BBC News. Retrieved from
http://news.bbc.co.uk/2/hi/europe/3091244.stm

20. Great Smog of '52

http://en.wikipedia.org/wiki/Great_Smog

http://en.wikipedia.org/wiki/Trams_in_London#Abandonment

Edinburgh University: The London Smog Disaster of 1952.
Retrieved from
http://www.portfolio.mvm.ed.ac.uk/studentwebs/session4/27/greatsmog52.htm

"Days of toxic darkness". BBC News. Retrieved from
http://news.bbc.co.uk/2/hi/uk_news/2542315.stm

"London fog clears after days of chaos". BBC News. Retrieved from http://news.bbc.co.uk/onthisday/hi/dates/stories/december/9/news id_4506000/4506390.stm

"50 Years On: The struggle for air quality in London since the great smog of December 1952" (Dec. 2002). Greater London Authority.

"The Great Smog of 1952". Retrieved from http://www.metoffice.gov.uk/learning/learn-about-the-weather/weather-phenomena/case-studies/great-smog

21. Cocoanut Grove Fire

http://en.wikipedia.org/wiki/Cocoanut_Grove_fire

http://www.cocoanutgrovefire.org/

"Cocoanut Grove Fire". With The Command Historical Perspective: U.S. Naval Academy Fire Department. Retrieved from http://www.withthecommand.com/2003-Aug/MD-tom-public1.html

http://www.celebrateboston.com/disasters/cocoanut-grove-fire.htm

http://www.bostonfirehistory.org/firestory11281942.html

http://www.cnn.com/2015/10/30/world/bucharest-nightclub-fire/

22. Disasters at the Hajj

http://en.wikipedia.org/wiki/Hajj

http://en.wikipedia.org/wiki/Incidents_during_the_Hajj

http://en.wikipedia.org/wiki/Stoning_of_the_Devil

http://en.wikipedia.org/wiki/Jamaraat_Bridge

"A history of hajj tragedies: World news". London. Retrieved from theguardian.com.

"Lessons from Hajj deaths". BBC News. Retrieved from News.bbc.co.uk.

"Millions descend on Mecca for haj". Retrieved from Iol.co.za.

"Hajj ritual sees new safety moves". BBC News, January 10, 2006.

Karimi, Faith; Ellis, Ralph; Hanna, Jason. "Crane collapse kills 107 people at mosque in Mecca days before Hajj". CNN. Retrieved from http://www.cnn.com/2015/09/12/middleeast/saudi-arabia-mecca-crane-collapse/

Karimi, Faith and Elwazer, Schams. "Stampede kills more than 700 at Hajj pilgrimage in Mecca". CNN, September 25, 2015. Retrieved from http://www.cnn.com/2015/09/24/middleeast/stampede-hajj-pilgrimage/

https://en.wikipedia.org/wiki/2015_Mina_stampede

23. Italian Hall Disaster

https://en.wikipedia.org/wiki/Italian_Hall_disaster

"Calumet, MI Theater Panic, Dec 1913". Retrieved from http://www3.gendisasters.com/michigan/2500/calumet-mi-theater-panic-dec-1913

http://www.huffingtonpost.com/steve-lehto/the-italian-hall-disaster_b_1120771.html

http://yoopersteez.com/post/italian-hall-disaster-1913

24. LeMans Crash

https://en.wikipedia.org/?title=1955_Le_Mans_disaster

https://en.wikipedia.org/wiki/1955_24_Hours_of_Le_Mans

"The SLR Phenomenon – Past and Future". Black Falcon Media Group. Retrieved from http://www.worldcarfans.com/104102510099/the-slr-phenomenon--past-and-future

http://www.ewilkins.com/wilko/lemans.htm

McMullen, Jeremy. "Mike Hawthorn & the 1955 24 Hours of Le Mans: The Cause and the Effect". Retrieved from http://www.conceptcarz.com/view/f1/teamsBySeason.aspx?driverTeamArticleID=160&driverID=65

25. Goiânia Radiological Contamination Accident

https://en.wikipedia.org/wiki/Goi%C3%A2nia_accident

Leite, Marco Antônio Sperb and Roper, L. David (1988) "The Goiânia Radiation Incident: A Failure of Science and Society". Retrieved from http://arts.bev.net/roperldavid/gri.htm

Foderaro, Lisa (July 8, 2010). "Columbia Scientists Prepare for a Threat: A Dirty Bomb". *The New York Times.* Retrieved from http://www.nytimes.com/2010/07/09/nyregion/09dirty.html?_r=0

"Aint No Way to Go: All That Glitters". Knight-Ridder, October 19, 1987. Retrieved from http://www.aintnowaytogo.com/glitter.htm

Irene, Mirelle (13 September 2012). "Goiânia, 25 anos depois: 'perguntam até se brilhamos', diz vítima Terra". Retrieved from http://noticias.terra.com.br/brasil/goiania-25-anos-depois-39perguntam-ate-se-brilhamos39-diz-vitima,bb12dc840f0da310VgnCLD200000bbcceb0aRCRD.html

26. Saint-Michel-de-Maurienne Derailment

https://en.wikipedia.org/wiki/Saint-Michel-de-Maurienne_derailment

"Modane, France (1917): The Worst Rail Accident Ever". Danger Ahead. Retrieved from http://danger-ahead.railfan.net/accidents/modane/home.html

27. Bhopal Gas Leak

http://en.wikipedia.org/wiki/Bhopal_disaster

Kalelkar AS, Little AD. (1998). "Investigation of Large-magnitude incidents: Bhopal as a Case Study". London: The Institution of Chemical Engineers Conference on Preventing Major Chemical Accidents.

Browning, Jackson B. (1993). "Union Carbide: Disaster at Bhopal".

http://www.bhopal.com/Cause-of-Bhopal-Tragedy

http://www.dailymail.co.uk/news/article-1284623/7-men-jailed-1984-Bhopal-gas-tragedy-killed-15-000-people.html

"Bhopal trial: Eight convicted over India gas disaster". BBC News. 7 June 2010.

28. Kyshtym Nuclear Disaster

https://en.wikipedia.org/wiki/Kyshtym_disaster

https://en.wikipedia.org/wiki/Lake_Karachay

Soran, Diane M.; Stillman, Danny B. (1982). "An Analysis of the Alleged Kyshtym Disaster". Los Alamos National Laboratory. Retrieved from http://www.iaea.org/inis/collection/NCLCollectionStore/_Public/14/724/14724059.pdf

http://www.nuclear-heritage.net/index.php/Kyshtym_Disaster

Collins, D.L. (1991). "Nuclear Accidents in the Former Soviet Union". Retrieved from http://www.dtic.mil/dtic/tr/fulltext/u2/a254669.pdf

29. SS *Eastland* Capsizing

https://en.wikipedia.org/wiki/SS_Eastland

http://www.chicagotribune.com/news/daywatch/chi-eastland-disaster-film-footage-20150208-htmlstory.html

http://www.eastlandmemorial.org/index.shtml

http://www.eastlanddisaster.org/history/what-happened

"The Eastland Disaster". WTTW. Retrieved from
http://www.wttw.com/main.taf?p=1,7,1,1,12

30. Sverdlovsk Anthrax Leak

https://en.wikipedia.org/wiki/Sverdlovsk_anthrax_leak

https://en.wikipedia.org/wiki/Yekaterinburg

http://www.pbs.org/wgbh/pages/frontline/shows/plague/sverdlovsk/

https://en.wikipedia.org/wiki/Dugway_sheep_incident

https://en.wikipedia.org/wiki/Biopreparat

Wampler, Robert A. and Blanton, Thomas S., ed. (November 15, 2001). "Anthrax at Sverdlovsk, 1979: U.S. Intelligence on the Deadliest Modern Outbreak". National Security Archive Electronic Briefing Book No. 61. Retrieved from http://nsarchive.gwu.edu/NSAEBB/NSAEBB61/

Science 1994, Volume 266, pp. 1202–1208. Retrieved from http://www.politicsandthelifesciences.org/Biosecurity_course_folder/readings/guillemin.pdf

31. San Juanico Explosions

https://en.wikipedia.org/wiki/San_Juanico_disaster

"PEMEX LPG Terminal, Mexico City, Mexico". 19 November 1984. Retrieved from http://www.hse.gov.uk/comah/sragtech/casepemex84.htm

"Reporte de Accidente de San Juan Ixhuatepec". Universidad de Zaragoza. Retrieved from http://www.unizar.es/guiar/1/Accident/San_Juan.htm

Arturson G., (April 1987). "The tragedy of San Juanico — the most severe LPG disaster in history". Retrieved from http://www.ncbi.nlm.nih.gov/pubmed/3580941

32. Rana Plaza Collapse

http://en.wikipedia.org/wiki/2013_Savar_building_collapse

"Bangladesh factory collapse: Clothes made for a tenth of retail price, documents show". *Toronto Star*, 14 May 2013. Retrieved from http://www.thestar.com/news/world/2013/05/14/bangladesh_factor y_collapse_clothes_made_for_a_tenth_of_retail_price_documents_ show.html

"A year after Rana Plaza: What hasn't changed since the Bangladesh factory collapse". *Washington Post*, 2014.04.18. Retrieved from http://www.washingtonpost.com/opinions/a-year-after-rana-plaza-what-hasnt-changed-since-the-bangladesh-factory-collapse/2014/04/18/9a06f266-c1c3-11e3-b195-dd0c1174052c_story.html

"Without stronger unions, Rana Plaza will happen time and time again". *The Guardian*. 24 April 2014. Retrieved from http://www.theguardian.com/global-development-professionals-network/2014/apr/24/rana-plaza-garment-workers-bangladesh

"27 Arrested at The Children's Place HQ in Protest over Factory Collapse". *Democracy Now!* 13 March 2015. Retrieved from http://www.democracynow.org/2015/3/13/headlines/27_arrested_a t_the_childrens_place_hq_in_protest_over_factory_collapse

http://news.biharprabha.com/2015/04/bangladesh-rana-plaza-incident-130-families-face-the-agony-of-missing-bodies/

33. Los Alfaques Explosion

https://en.wikipedia.org/wiki/Los_Alfaques_disaster

https://en.wikipedia.org/wiki/Right_to_be_forgotten

Anderson, Nate (February 12, 2012). "Spain asks: If Google search results make your business look bad, can you sue?". *Ars Technica.* Retrieved from http://arstechnica.com/tech-policy/2012/02/spain-asks-if-google-search-results-make-your-business-look-bad-can-you-sue/

"It Was Like Napalm." *Time*, July 24, 1978. Retrieved from

http://content.time.com/time/magazine/article/0,9171,946862,00.ht
ml

Ramiro, J.M. Santamaría; Aísa, P.A. Braña. "Risk Analysis and
Reduction in the Chemical Process Industry". *Science*, 2012

"Holiday That Turned Into Hell". Google News. Retrieved from
https://news.google.com/newspapers?nid=1300&dat=19780713&id
=0eZaAAAAIBAJ&sjid=TpIDAAAAIBAJ&pg=3703,5543767&hl=en

34. Sinking of the *Wilhelm Gustloff*

https://en.wikipedia.org/wiki/MV_Wilhelm_Gustloff

https://en.wikipedia.org/wiki/List_of_ships_sunk_by_submarines_
by_death_toll

http://www.wilhelmgustloff.com/history_escapeship.htm

Kappes, Irwin J. (2003). "The Greatest Marine Disaster in
History...and why you probably never heard of it". Retrieved from
http://www.militaryhistoryonline.com/wwii/articles/wilhelmgustl
off.aspx

Sellwood, A.V. "The Damned Don't Drown: The Sinking of the
Wilhelm Gustloff". Retrieved from
http://www.feldgrau.com/wilhelmgustloff.html

35. Yellow River Flood and Changsha Fire

https://en.wikipedia.org/wiki/Second_Sino-Japanese_War

https://en.wikipedia.org/wiki/1938_Yellow_River_flood

Lary, Diana (1 April 2001). "Drowned Earth: The Strategic
Breaching of the Yellow River Dyke, 1938". *War in History.*

https://en.wikipedia.org/wiki/Chiang_Kai-shek

"1938 China." MSN encarta. 6 Jan 2007. Retrieved from
http://www.webcitation.org/query?id=1256961934128781

36. Hyatt Regency Hotel Walkway Collapse

https://en.wikipedia.org/wiki/Hyatt_Regency_walkway_collapse

Marshall, Richard D. et al. (May 1982). "Investigation of the Kansas City Hyatt Regency walkways collapse". Building Science Series 143. U.S. Dept. of Commerce, National Bureau of Standards.

"Hyatt Regency Walkway Collapse". Engineering.com. Retrieved from http://www.engineering.com/Library/ArticlesPage/tabid/85/article Type/ArticleView/articleId/175/Walkway-Collapse.aspx

Associated Press (July 15, 2001). "Lives forever changed by skywalk collapse". *Lawrence Journal World* (Lawrence, KS: LJWorld.com). Retrieved from http://www2.ljworld.com/news/ 2001/jul/15/lives_forever_changed/

"Disaster made heroes of the helpers". *Kansas City Star*. Retrieved from http://skywalk.kansascity.com/articles/disaster-made-heroes-helpers/

McGuire, Donna. "20 years later: Fatal disaster remains impossible to forget". *Kansas City Star*. Retrieved from http://skywalk.kansascity.com/articles/20-years-later-fatal-disaster-remains-impossible-forget/

Montgomery, Rick (July 15, 2001). "20 years later: Many are continuing to learn from skywalk collapse". *Kansas City Star*. Retrieved from http://skywalk.kansascity.com/articles/20-years-later-many-are-continuing-learn-skywalk-collapse//

37. Kursha-2 Firestorm

https://en.wikipedia.org/wiki/Kursha-2

https://en.wikipedia.org/wiki/Firestorm

https://en.wikipedia.org/wiki/Fire_whirl

https://en.wikipedia.org/wiki/Black_Saturday_bushfires

http://meljay.hubpages.com/hub/Recent-Natural-Disasters-the-Worst-Fires

38. *Le Joola* Ferry Capsizing

https://en.wikipedia.org/wiki/MV_Le_Joola

"Hundreds lost as Senegal ferry sinks". BBC News. September 27, 2002. Retrieved from http://news.bbc.co.uk/2/hi/africa/2285092.stm

"Q&A: What caused the Joola ferry disaster?". BBC News. October 1, 2002. Retrieved from http://news.bbc.co.uk/2/hi/africa/2290490.stm

"Senegal army 'left' ferry survivors". BBC News. November 6, 2002. Retrieved from http://news.bbc.co.uk/2/hi/africa/2409087.stm

"Report blames army for delay in Joola rescue". IRIN. November 6, 2002. Retrieved from http://www.irinnews.org/report/35577/senegal-report-blames-army-for-delay-in-joola-rescue

Jullien, Maud. "Africa's Titanic: Seeking justice a decade after Joola". BBC News. September 26 , 2012. Retrieved from http://www.bbc.com/news/world-africa-19717929

Ramirez, Luis (November 4, 2002). "Senegal President Dismisses Prime Minister". Voice of America. Retrieved from http://www.voanews.com/content/a-13-a-2002-11-04-32-senegal/392010.html

"Senegal Marks Anniversary of Ferry Disaster Amid Court Cases". Voice of America. September 26, 2008. Retrieved from http://www.voanews.com/content/a-13-2008-09-26-voa39/400523.html

39. Texas City Explosions

https://en.wikipedia.org/wiki/Texas_City_disaster

"Fire on the Grandcamp". Moore Memorial Public Library. Retrieved from http://www.texascity-library.org/disaster/fire.php

"Texas City, Texas Disaster". Fire Prevention and Engineering Bureau of Texas. April 29, 1947. Retrieved from http://www.local1259iaff.org/report.htm

"Blasts and Fires Wreck Texas City of 15,000; 300 to 1,200 Dead; Thousands Hurt, Homeless; Wide Coast Area Rocked, Damage in Millions". *New York Times*. April 17, 1947. Retrieved from http://www.nytimes.com/learning/general/onthisday/big/0416.htm l#article

Lienhard, John H. (1996). "Engines of our Ingenuity: No. 1138: The Texas City Disaster." Radio broadcast: University of Houston. Retrieved from http://www.uh.edu/engines/epi1138.htm

http://www.cityofroseburg.org/visitors/1959-blast/

https://en.wikipedia.org/wiki/West_Fertilizer_Company_explosio n

https://en.wikipedia.org/wiki/Texas_City_Refinery_explosion

https://en.wikipedia.org/wiki/2015_Tianjin_explosions

40. Zolitūde Shopping Center Collapse

https://en.wikipedia.org/wiki/Zolit%C5%ABde_shopping_centre_r oof_collapse

McGuinness, Damien (23 November 2013). "Remaining section of Latvia supermarket roof collapses." BBC News. Retrieved from http://www.bbc.com/news/world-europe-25068291

"Riga supermarket collapse death toll reaches 53 people, rescuers have 150 m 2 of debris left to be combed". The Voice of Russia. 23 November 2013. Retrieved from http://sputniknews.com/voiceofrussia/news/2013_11_23/Riga-supermarket-collapse-death-toll-reaches-53-people-rescuers-have-150-m-2-of-debris-left-to-be-combed-9220/

Sabet-Parry, Rayyan (24 November 2013). "LATEST: Rescue mission comes to an end at supermarket collapse site". RIGA, Latvia: Baltictimes.com. Retrieved from http://www.baltictimes.com/news/articles/33818/#.UpPzGcTIZ2k

"At least 53 dead after Latvia mall collapse". RT. 21 November 2013. Retrieved from http://www.rt.com/news/riga-mall-collapse-latvia-118/

41. Ufa Train Disaster

https://en.wikipedia.org/wiki/Ufa_train_disaster

"Russia remembers 1989 Ufa train disaster". RIA Novosti. 2009-06-04. Retrieved from http://sputniknews.com/russia/20090604/155167464.html

http://en.atropedia.net/article:384fd5

Keller, Bill (June 5, 1989). "500 on 2 Trains Reported Killed By Soviet Gas Pipeline Explosion". *New York Times*. Retrieved from http://www.nytimes.com/1989/06/05/world/500-on-2-trains-reported-killed-by-soviet-gas-pipeline-explosion.html

42. *Doña Paz* Ferry Sinking

https://en.wikipedia.org/wiki/MV_Do%C3%B1a_Paz

"Sulpicio Lines vessels in major marine mishaps". GMA News Online. June 24, 2008. Retrieved from http://www.gmanetwork.com/news/story/102786/news/sulpicio-lines-vessels-in-major-marine-mishaps

Caltex Philippines v. Sulpicio Lines, 374 Phil. 325 (Supreme Court of the Philippines), 1999-09-30. Retrieved from http://www.lawphil.net/judjuris/juri1999/sep1999/gr_131166_1999.html

"1,500 Are Feared Lost as 2 Ships Collide and Sink Near Philippines". Associated Press. December 21, 1987. Retrieved from http://www.nytimes.com/1987/12/21/world/1500-are-feared-lost-as-2-ships-collide-and-sink-near-philippines.html

Coronel, Sheila S. "Searchers Find No Trace of 1,500 From 2 Ships Sunk in Philippines". *New York Times*. December 22, 1987. Retrieved from http://www.nytimes.com/1987/12/22/world/searchers-find-no-trace-of-1500-from-2-ships-sunk-in-philippines.html

"Officers Were Not at Posts, Ship Disaster Survivor Says". AP. December 25, 1987. Retrieved from http://www.nytimes.com/1987/12/25/world/officers-were-not-at-posts-ship-disaster-survivor-says.html

43. New London School Explosion

https://en.wikipedia.org/wiki/New_London_School_explosion

"The London Museum on the Web!" Retrieved from http://web.archive.org/web/20060108194036/http://www.westrusk.esc7.net/lmuseum/building.html

New London School Disaster Explosion. Retrieved from http://www.hilliard.ws/nlondon.htm

New London School Explosion. Retrieved from nlsd.net

Texas Board of Professional Engineers: An Inventory of Board of Professional Engineers Records at the Texas State Archives, 1937, 1952, 1972-2001, 2005-2006, undated. Retrieved from http://www.lib.utexas.edu/taro/tslac/50009/tsl-50009.html

Turner, Allan (2012-03-11). "Memories still vivid 75 years after school explosion". *Houston Chronicle*. Retrieved from http://www.chron.com/news/houston-texas/article/Memories-still-vivid-75-years-after-school-3397237.php

Stowers, Carlton (February 21, 2002). "Today, a generation died". *Dallas Observer*. Retrieved from http://www.dallasobserver.com/news/today-a-generation-died-6390526

44. Shiloh Baptist Church Panic

https://en.wikipedia.org/wiki/Shiloh_Baptist_Church_disaster

https://en.wikipedia.org/wiki/Booker_T._Washington

"Hundred Fifteen Killed". *Boston Evening Transcript*, September 20, 1902. Retrieved from https://news.google.com/newspapers?nid=2249&dat=19020920&id=wYU-AAAAIBAJ&sjid=IVoMAAAAIBAJ&pg=6271,2347342&hl=en

"Negro dead number 115. No white people killed in the Birmingham panic". *The New York Times*, New York 1902-09-21. Retrieved from http://www3.gendisasters.com/alabama/2451/birmingham,-al-baptist-church-disaster,-sept-1902

Garrison, Greg (October 23, 2010). "Historic Greater Shiloh Missionary Baptist moving West End neighborhood forward". Retrieved from http://blog.al.com/living-news/2010/10/historic_greater_shiloh_missio.html

45. Palace of the Grand Master Explosion

https://dailydisaster.wordpress.com/2009/04/03/april-3-1856-palace-of-the-grand-masters-explosion-rhodes/

https://en.wikipedia.org/wiki/Palace_of_the_Grand_Master_of_the_Knights_of_Rhodes

http://hubpages.com/hub/Rhodes-Greece-The-Palace-of-the-Grand-Master

Spignesi, Stephen J. "Catastrophe!: The 100 Greatest Disasters Of All Time". Citadel Press, 2004.

46. Peshtigo Fire

Ball, Jacqueline A. "Wildfire! The 1871 Peshtigo Firestorm". New York: Bearport Pub., 2005.

https://en.wikipedia.org/wiki/Peshtigo_Fire

https://en.wikipedia.org/wiki/Green_Island_Light_(Wisconsin)

DeLaluzern, Guillaume (Oct. 1871). "IN WISCONSIN. Particulars of the Burning of Williamsonville and Peshtigo — Frightful Number of Deaths". Peshtigo, WI: *Green Bay Wisconsin Advocate*. Retrieved from http://www3.gendisasters.com/wisconsin/8616/peshtigo-wi-great-peshtigo-fire-oct-1871

Geyer, Rev. Kurt (October 6, 1921). "History of the Peshtigo fire,

October 8, 1871". *Peshtigo Times*. Retrieved from
http://www.wisconsinhistory.org/Content.aspx?dsNav=N:4294963
828-4294963788&dsRecordDetails=R:BA13523

Biondich, S. (2010-06-09). "The Great Peshtigo Fire".
ExpressMilwaukee.com. Shepherd Express. Retrieved from
http://expressmilwaukee.com/article-11172-the-great-peshtigo-
fire.html

https://en.wikipedia.org/wiki/Shrine_of_Our_Lady_of_Good_Hel
p

https://en.wikipedia.org/wiki/Great_Chicago_Fire

47.Lagos Armory Explosion

https://en.wikipedia.org/wiki/Lagos_armoury_explosion

"Nigeria military under fire". BBC. 29 January 2002. Retrieved
from http://news.bbc.co.uk/2/hi/africa/1787494.stm

"Lagos blasts leave 600 dead". BBC. 28 January 2002. Retrieved
from http://news.bbc.co.uk/2/hi/africa/1786465.stm

"Toll blast at Nigerian armoury exceeds 1,000". *New York Times*. 3
February 2002. Retrieved from
http://www.nytimes.com/2002/02/03/world/toll-in-blast-at-
nigerian-armory-exceeds-1000.html

"Lagos explosions leave 100 dead". BBC. 28 January 2002.
Retrieved from http://news.bbc.co.uk/2/hi/africa/1785571.stm

"Armoury Explosion In Lagos, Nigeria" World Health
Organization. Retrieved from
http://www.afro.who.int/en/nigeria/press-materials/item/380-
armoury-explosion-in-lagos-nigeria.html

48. Galveston Hurricane

Larson, Erik. "Isaac's Storm: A Man, A Time, and the Deadliest
Hurricane in History" (1st ed.). New York: Crown Publishers,
1999.

https://en.wikipedia.org/wiki/1900_Galveston_hurricane

"Galveston 1900: Storm of the Century". The Portal to Texas History. Retrieved from http://education.texashistory.unt.edu/lessons/psa/Galveston1900/

"The 1900 Storm — Galveston Island, Texas — Remembering the Great Hurricane". September 8, 1900. A *Galveston County Daily News* Presentation. Retrieved from http://www.1900storm.com/

"Galveston Hurricane of 1900 Texas". Archive of the Moving Image. Retrieved from http://www.texasarchive.org/library/index.php/Category:Galveston_Hurricane_of_1900

Garriott, E. B. (October 1900). "The West Indian Hurricane Of September 1–12, 1900". *National Geographic Magazine* XI (10): 384–392. Retrieved from https://books.google.com/books?id=9g4OAQAAIAAJ&pg=PA384&hl=en#v=onepage&q&f=false

Lienhard, John H. "Raising Galveston". The Engines of Our Ingenuity. University of Houston. Retrieved from http://www.uh.edu/engines/epi865.htm

Moore, Willis L. (October 1900). "The Weather Bureau and the Gulf Storms". *The National Magazine* XIII (1): 542–546. Retrieved from https://books.google.com/books?id=9o7NAAAAMAAJ&pg=PA542&hl=en#v=onepage&q&f=false

49. Chernobyl Nuclear Disaster

https://en.wikipedia.org/wiki/Chernobyl_disaster

https://en.wikipedia.org/wiki/Glasnost

https://en.wikipedia.org/wiki/Chernobyl_Nuclear_Power_Plant_sarcophagus

https://en.wikipedia.org/wiki/Chernobyl_New_Safe_Confinement

International Chernobyl Portal of the ICRIN Project. Retrieved from http://chernobyl.info/en-US/Home/History-of-Chernobyl-

Disaster.aspx

"Chernobyl—The Lost Film". Retrieved from
https://www.youtube.com/watch?v=NkjAAzkrXSA

"Chernobyl: The Victims". Retrieved from
http://www.gerdludwig.com/stories/chernobyl-the-
victims/#id=album-12&num=content-48

"Chernobyl Cleanup: No End In Sight". Retrieved from
http://www.gerdludwig.com/recent-work/chernobyl-cleanup-no-
end-in-sight/#id=album-9&num=content-5

"Chernobyl: The Exclusion Zone". Retrieved from
http://www.gerdludwig.com/stories/chernobyl-the-exclusion-
zone/#id=album-11&num=content-30

"Environmental Consequences of the Chernobyl Accident and
Their Remediation: Twenty Years of Experience". Report of the
Chernobyl Forum Expert Group 'Environment', International
Atomic Energy Agency, Vienna, 2006. Retrieved from http://www-
pub.iaea.org/MTCD/publications/PDF/Pub1239_web.pdf

50. Great Kantō Earthquake

https://en.wikipedia.org/wiki/1923_Great_Kant%C5%8D_earthqua
ke

https://en.wikipedia.org/wiki/Yokoamicho_Park

"The Great Kantō earthquake of 1923". Retrieved from
http://www.greatkantoearthquake.com/

"Great Tokyo Earthquake of 1923: Facts and Details". Retrieved
from http://factsanddetails.com/japan/cat26/sub160/item2226.html

Hammer, Joshua. "The Great Japan Earthquake of 1923".
Smithsonian Magazine, May 2011. Retrieved from
http://www.smithsonianmag.com/history/the-great-japan-
earthquake-of-1923-1764539/?no-ist

Neff, Robert (2006-09-29). "The Great Kanto Earthquake
Massacre". Retrieved from
http://english.ohmynews.com/articleview/article_view.asp?menu=

c10400&no=320400&rel_no=1

Helibrun, Jacob (September 17, 2006). "Aftershocks". *The New York Times*. Retrieved from http://www.nytimes.com/2006/09/17/books/review/Heilbrunn.t.html?_r=0

"The Great Kanto Earthquake of 1923". Library.brown.edu. Retrieved from http://library.brown.edu/cds/kanto/denewa.html

James, Charles. "The 1923 Tokyo Earthquake and Fire". University of California, Berkeley, 2002.10.08. Retrieved from http://nisee.berkeley.edu/kanto/tokyo1923.pdf

http://learni.st/users/580/boards/37914-fire-tornadoes-the-great-kanto-earthquake

About the Author

Mr. King holds degrees from the University of Wisconsin-Madison in History, Geography, and Social Studies Education. He lives with his wife and family in suburban Madison, Wisconsin. He loves to research and re-tell the stories of obscure and nearly forgotten historical events, and to create new alternative-history stories.

Made in the USA
Charleston, SC
18 March 2016